Bringing Out the Best in Students

Bringing Out the Best in Students

How Legendary Teachers Motivate Kids

David Scheidecker

William Freeman

CORWIN PRESS, INC.
A Sage Publications Company
Thousand Oaks, California

For information:

Corwin Press, Inc.
A Sage Publications Company
2455 Teller Road
Thousand Oaks, California 91320
E-mail: order@corwinpress.com

SAGE Publications Ltd.
6 Bonhill Street
London EC2A 4PU
United Kingdom

SAGE Publications India Pvt. Ltd.
M-32 Market
Greater Kailash I
New Delhi 110 048 India

Printed in the United States of America

Library of Congress Cataloging-in-Publication Data

Scheidecker, David, 1950-
  Bringing out the best in students: How legendary teachers
motivate kids/by David Scheidecker and William Freeman.
    p. cm.
  ISBN 0-8039-6756-X (cloth: acid-free paper)
  ISBN 0-8039-6757-8 (pbk: acid-free paper)
  1. Motivation in education. 2. Effective teaching. I. Freeman,
William, 1951-   II. Title.
  LB1065.S344 1998
  370.15′4—dc21   98-40268

This book is printed on acid-free paper.

00 01 02 03 04 10 9 8 7 6 5 4 3 2

Corwin Editorial Assistant: Julia Parnell
Production Editor: Denise Santoyo
Editorial Assistant: Nevair Kabakian
Designer/Typesetter: Danielle Dillahunt
Cover Designer: Tracy E. Miller

CONTENTS

PREFACE

> *Everyone knows a legend—the teacher who is successful at bringing out the best in students, regardless of the location of the school, the diversity of the students, the conditions of the facilities, or the availability of resources. At least one legend can be found in every school. This is a book about the characteristics that define the legendary teacher, about how you can recognize and acknowledge those characteristics in teachers, and about how you can foster the development of those characteristics in yourself and colleagues. Throughout the book, you will find hundreds of examples and strategies for becoming a legend.*

We're into the second century of American public education, and if the press is at all correct, we haven't become much better at it. In fact, many people think we've gotten worse.

Nevertheless, referendums continue to be defeated; facilities continue to be neglected; and state and federal dollars continue to disappear. At the very same time, however, curricula continue to grow as education is given more and more responsibility to cure society's ills. Traditional families are a thing of the past, as, apparently, is school authority. (In *loco parentis* has gone from meaning "in place of the parent" to "the parents are crazy too!") The situation has so deteriorated that it seems that sometimes decisions are no longer based on what is best for the students but what is legalistically tenable. Left all alone in the front lines is the classroom teacher.

Even more surprising than the litany of what's wrong with public education today is that some teachers not only succeed in this environment, they thrive. There is probably not a school in America where there is not, at least, one teacher who continues to make a difference in the lives of children. Despite the financial pinch, despite the lack of support from a graying population, despite the changing demographics of the community, there is at least that one teacher who makes everything work, who inspires the slow learner, who challenges the gifted, who somehow gets the problem student focused successfully on learning. Where other teachers have struggled, this one succeeds. The programs and activities this teacher sponsors thrive while other programs shrivel and wither away.

The community is well aware of this teacher as well. At registration time, parents often pray, "I hope my child gets _____ this year!" Somehow, in spite of all that is wrong with education today, this one teacher has earned the respect of the students (who otherwise don't like classes), the school (that would require forms for breathing if it could), and even the community (that somehow believes schools have existed in a vacuum untouched by inflation since the 1960s). This teacher has become what this book is about, a legend.

Legends are life touchers. They are the reason students want to come to class every day. In a time when role models are in decline elsewhere, legends shine brightly, daily exemplifying their values, making things work. This book is dedicated to those legends, to examining what they have that makes them so preeminent in their profession, that makes them so important to the lives of so many children.

This book is broken down, chapter by chapter, into what we think makes legends legendary in their schools. We do not suggest that what is presented is causal in nature; rather, we see those characteristics described as correlative to successful teaching. They seem to be pretty much unvarying among the most successful teachers regardless of locale or grade level.

Chapter 1, "Piecing Together the Personality Puzzle," discusses the character traits, attitudes, and habits of legendary teachers. In

Chapter 2, "Nothing Succeeds Like Success," we present the strategies that legends use to ensure student success. Chapter 3, "Establishing High Expectations," describes methods of establishing high expectations for student performance and helping students to meet those expectations. In Chapter 4, "Practicing Skillful Communication," we enumerate ways of effectively communicating with students, parents, community members, and colleagues. Chapter 5, "From Chaos to Organization," shows how legends organize time, space, and the varied multiple tasks of daily teaching. Chapter 6, "Recognizing and Promoting Excellence," discusses ways of promoting student excellence through recognition of student achievement. In Chapter 7, "Motiviating High Student Achievement," we present many strategies for motivating the reluctant learner. Chapter 8, "Developing Powerful Classroom Management Skills," addresses the perennial problem of sustaining a positive learning environment through effective classroom management strategies. Chapter 9, "Becoming a Legend," summarizes what it means to be a legendary teacher.

Is it possible for any teacher to become a legend? The question, because it is so hypothetical, is virtually meaningless, but what is meaningful is the belief that by careful study of the characteristics of these legends, every teacher can improve his or her effectiveness in the classroom, his or her ability to be a life toucher. Whether you will be a success in the classroom, whether you make a difference in a child's life, whether you become a legend depends on one thing and one thing only—you.

Our hope for this book is clearly presented in Figure i.1.

Before turning you loose into our book, we'd like to share a simple experience we had. One of our better friends was the plant manager of a General Food plant that manufactures Gaines dog food. He was an important man in town and handsomely rewarded for his efforts, six figures annually at a time we had just broken the five-figure barrier.

On many weekends, we would meet him at his house before heading out to one of several local golf courses. Weekend after weekend, we'd get to his house only to have to wait, impatiently, for him to get there. He'd be doing volunteer work at the YMCA or setting up a youth basketball program or arranging visits to hospitals; nonetheless, we'd wait until he got home—he, apparently failing to realize that our time set aside to play golf was, at least in our minds, sacrosanct.

S
T
E
P

1

We are not foolish enough to believe that we can produce for you a simple six-step method for achieving teaching excellence. That, of course, would be gross oversimplification. But we do believe their exists a set of correlatives shared by many teaching legends and that conscious knowledge of those correlatives may indeed lead to more effective teaching.

Individual teachers must be attuned to what works for them, what fits their teaching methods—for teaching, more so than any other profession, is about individualized style. Legends find their own stride, are in harmony with the rhythm of their classes. There are no simple answers, no quick fixes.

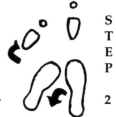

S
T
E
P

2

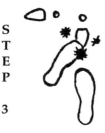

S
T
E
P

3

Instead of giving you a new teaching protocol, a new paradigm, we suggest instead that you invent your own, and that doing so is made easier by the suggestions presented within this book. Our belief is that every classroom success is its own invention.

So, we invite you to be creative—we invite you to invent or reinvent yourself. We think what we have to offer will make that imminently possible. We, like you, are makers of people, and we challenge you to make the best people you can, by being the best teacher you are able to be. It is the world's most important challenge.

S
T
E
P

4

Figure i.1. The Dance

Finally, on a Saturday when he made us wait almost an hour, we cornered him, "What's with all this charity work? This is golf day—remember?"

"Well, guys," he responded looking only a little guilty, "I'm not like you—I'm not a teacher, and whenever I get a chance I have to try to do something of value to put some meaning in my life."

That is the sentiment we hold most dearly.

This book is written for people we believe do some of the most meaningful work on earth, the education of children.

The thoughtful and detailed advice of the following reviewers is gratefully acknowledged:

John Daresh, University of Texas, El Paso

Rick Heidt, Bismark High School, Bismark, North Dakota

Laurel LeBoeuf, Child and Family Resource Center, Canandaigua, New York

ABOUT THE AUTHORS

David Scheidecker has been a high school English teacher for 27 years: 20 of them as the head of an English department. His professional activities include serving as a reader for the Advanced Placement English Literature and Composition exam; acting as a consultant to the college board; hosting seminars for Advanced Placement teachers; and consulting with various high schools in terms of professional inservice, curriculum design, evaluation technique, and miscellaneous instructional concerns. Scheidecker has worked extensively in curriculum design and revision at his own high school. In addition, he has served as a high school baseball, football, and wrestling coach; as a class sponsor; as the director of dramatics and forensics; and as the head of a high school mentor program. He also was recognized as a "Teacher of Merit" by the state school board of Illinois.

William Freeman has 11 years of teaching experience in a middle school social studies department. He has spent the past 15 years as a high school principal. In addition to his administrative duties, he is a North-Central Accreditation facilitator and has been president of a county administrators' association and an athletic conference. He is a trained administrative analyst and has written gifted curriculum for junior high school social studies classes. He has also served as a junior high school athletic director; baseball, basketball, and track coach; class sponsor; play director; and student council adviser. Freeman is a clever and frequent motivational keynote speaker at graduations, student assemblies, leadership conferences, and inservices, with a special area of expertise in effective instructional techniques and strategies in the classroom.

To our wives, Kathy and Carol, and our children, Damian, Kelly, Mindra, and Seth, who have always encouraged us throughout our educational careers to become the best that we could be. We would never have had the time to grow professionally as "life toucher" teachers/administrators without your support, sacrifice, and love.

Thank you for always being by our sides.

PIECING TOGETHER
THE PERSONALITY PUZZLE

The chicken-and-egg dilemma has its parallel in education. It is the question of whether good teachers are born or if they are made: the nature versus nurture question. Our answer to that controversy is, fittingly, an enigma itself. Generally speaking, we believe good teachers are born, but more important, we believe it's better for everyone involved if we were to believe that they could be made. Interestingly, this book is predicated on a rejection of the question. The question is rather moot. What is relevant is the belief that there are traits, even personality character traits, that anyone can improve on to enhance his or her effectiveness as a master teacher, as a legend.

Personality is generally defined as the set of an individual's distinguishing character traits, attitudes, and habits. Looking more deeply into the definition, one can clearly see that personality is the single most significant feature that distinguishes one individual from another individual or, in the setting of the school, one teacher's success from another's. There are certainly as many types of personalities as there are teachers in any given school system, and just as obviously, there is no single, specific type of teacher personality or trait that could be classified as preferable in all situations all the time.

But there are instructors, legends in education, who seem to have the personalities most able to make a difference in the lives of children on a daily basis.

Before getting into the personality components of a legend, one must first be ready to master the interpersonal skills that will allow him or her to open all the possible venues for educational excellence. In this first chapter, we focus on the three parts of the definition that clearly distinguish the legend's personality from that of his or her less successful peers: character traits, strong attitudes, and good habits.

A COMMON SCENARIO

Reality Sets In

The hands on the face of the clock in the classroom seem to be stuck; a persistent fear drifts in and out of the young teacher's mind, "What am I doing here? Why did I become a teacher?" As she looks at the pile of papers she will have to tackle at home that evening, after she has supervised a home basketball game, after she's fixed supper for her family, and after she's helped her husband do the dishes, she begins to understand why her all-knowing parents responded with a quizzical "Teacher?" when she told them what career path she had decided to follow. Just about the time she has absolutely had it with the negative attitude of two especially aggravating students in her fourth-period class, the bell rings, saving both her and the students from what could only be a mutually destructive confrontation. Now at least she has lunch, a 30-minute duty-free time slot, her only respite from the intellectual wrestling others call "teaching."

The Shock

As she enters the cafeteria, the teacher is overwhelmed by a sea of children, each of whom is either screaming at someone or pushing someone else (and for the overachievers—both). The noise is deafening; she accelerates her pace so that she can get quickly through the cafeteria line and gulp down her Tylenol-laced lunch in the teacher's lounge, in hopes of quelling the acidic buildup of her stomach and the throbbing veins of her forehead.

As she battles her way into the lunch line, the teacher is taken aback by the sight of two renegades from her last class standing in line engaging in polite conversation with another teacher—and no, he's not a coach! As she pauses to take in this image (which suddenly seems to have theological implications), her feelings move from wonder

—"How does he do that?"

to awe

—"Look, they're smiling!"

to anger

—"Why don't they treat me that way?"

and finally to suspicion

—"Who is this guy and what did he do?"

An Epiphany of Sorts

As the conversation continues, despite her resentment, the teacher can't help but be aware of the positive interaction that is occurring, and unwillingly (and perhaps even unconsciously) she begins to wonder how any teacher could ever have a relationship with those two students. Turning away from the conversation, she enters the lunch line, gets her food, and heads toward the faculty lounge with a pair of queries riddling her mind: "What kind of meat is this really?" and, most important, "What do those two students see in that teacher that I don't have?"

The answer is probably not a better pedagogy; the answer is probably not a more interesting curriculum; the answer is probably not a more modern technology; the answer is probably not that the teacher she witnessed is a "pushover" in the classroom. Instead, the answer (and this is not necessarily a terrible thing for her to come to grips with) is personality. For our discussion, we have chosen to break down the larger concept of personality into four areas:

- A disclaimer
- Identifying desirable character traits
- Promoting strong attitudes
- Developing good habits

A DISCLAIMER

Admittedly, this is not a very impressive way to start a book on education, but as we moved this chapter from our brains on to the page, the scenario troubled us greatly because the first few drafts sounded as though they were presenting a panacea to education, and although we don't believe in panaceas, we do believe in education.

What bothered us as we considered personality was the adage that opposites attract. If that's true, and there are a zillion types of personalities (which is, incidentally, about as close to mathematical analysis as we get in this work), then the sad truth is that no one teacher's personality could ever appeal to every type of student. Follow this logic:

- It must be assumed that each student brings to class a very different personality of his or her own and very distinct set of needs.
- It also must be assumed that every teacher can fill those needs to some degree.
- It is, however, impossible for any single teacher to present a personality that will be attractive to all students.

But while admitting that no individual teacher can have a personality that is naturally attractive to all students, one must recognize that every teacher can make certain that his or her personality does not include any traits that would preclude learning for any students. Although not everyone will become a teacher's friend, it is safe to assume that none need become the teacher's enemy. That simple observation is why we chose to begin this book with a discussion of personality: The teacher's personality is the single most significant trait in promoting educational success. The teacher is more important to the education of his or her students than pedagogy, technology, curriculum, facilities, and textbooks.

How does one's personality become the key to opening the door to touching the lives of students? We return to the question of whether legends are born or made; as we suggested earlier, it is in the best interest of education to operate under the assumption that they are not born—that it is possible for every teacher to nurture personality traits that will help him or her establish an environment more conducive for learning for all students. This then is our next task—an examination of aspects of a teacher's personality that are most conducive to student success.

IDENTIFYING DESIRABLE CHARACTER TRAITS

Almost every adult in America can identify a special or favorite teacher who had a tremendously positive effect on his or her life. Each of us looks back to that one teacher who motivated us, cared for us, taught us, and helped us to grow more than the others. When asked to identify a few phrases that best describe their favorite teacher, most adults' lists include the following:

- Informed
- Creative
- Compassionate
- Understanding
- Interesting
- Patient
- Honest
- Even tempered

- Happy
- Motivated
- Different
- Intense
- Exciting
- Positive
- Challenging
- Dedicated

- Encouraging
- Funny
- Fair

- Friendly
- Nonthreatening
- Caring

We all know that the teacher who can exhibit even half of these traits any time after the middle of September can walk on water—but for the rest of us, this list of descriptors can be broken down into four major areas of concerns students really have about those who direct their education.

Concern 1: **Surveys Appear to Suggest That Students Seem to Be Attracted to Classrooms Where the Instruction Is Informed Yet Entertaining ("creative," "funny," "friendly," "interesting," "happy," and "different")**

Students are not always looking for the easy way out. We all know they won't completely understand that concept until somewhere in the middle of their junior year in college. By and large, they do wish to learn and tend to respect the teacher who makes learning enjoyable. The legend's classroom is exciting. Students are challenged to do well, in the expectation that they will. The coordination of instruction, practice, and remediation prior to measurement is such that interested students can and do succeed. The legend's classroom looks and feels different from the other classrooms of the school.

When one enters this room, he or she knows that what follows is categorically different from the other experiences of the day. It is a fun place where learning occurs. In this classroom, humor is as prevalent as content. The fun is what makes learning easy. The legend may present material with a comedic sense. The presentation does not dissolve into stand-up comedy, but there is great deal of appropriate laughter intermingled with a wide variety of learning activities. How clearly can we say it—learning is fun here.

Humor can be used in a mnemonic fashion: "The House of Tudor can be remembered as a house that, because it had

to accommodate both the warring families of the Yorks and
Lancasters, had to have two doors: that's how I remember
it still."

Humor can be used in a self-deprecating manner: "My
penmanship was so poor when I was a student teacher, my
college professor made me take the class on writing on the
board three times, but I finally learned it—you can too."

Humor can be used anecdotally: "My freshman biology
teacher had to help me remember what the fifth characteristic of a mammal was, and he did it by standing by my
desk, pulling the hair on my arm, until I finally guessed—
'Fur?' "

The legend doesn't rely on gimmicks: There is no list of clever
activities that can be memorized, no definitive source of entertain-
ment, but the successful teacher does seek to make the learning
experience enjoyable, interactive, and original. The teacher's personality and planning make this possible.

Having just suggested that no list of activities, no specific approach can be shared that would not soon becomes as stale as any
other material, we must also say that there is an attitude about the
classroom experience that can be shared.

One of our student teachers was not having a great deal of
success once she took over the class. The students begged the
supervising teacher to come back because, they said, they
weren't learning anything; they had trouble forcing themselves
to pay attention. The supervising teacher was empathetic to
their feelings, but was not prepared to tell the student teacher
that she was boring. He was prepared to make suggestions
about lesson plans, closure, individualizing instruction—but not
about how to be interesting.

Matters grew steadily worse; the student teacher began
experiencing some behavior problems. One day after school,
the supervising teacher told her they needed to talk. They both
sat down at a table, the silence slightly awkward until he finally
asked her, "So, how do you think it's going?"

The student teacher paused for a moment and then said, "I didn't know you had to put a show on every day for these kids, and honestly, I don't think I have my act together . . . yet."

Despite her present shortcomings, it was at that moment that the supervising teacher knew she'd be all right.

***Concern 2:* Students Look for a Learning Environment That Challenges Them to Learn But Is Safe From Ridicule and Failure ("informed," "patient," "nonthreatening," "motivated," "challenging" "encouraging," and "positive")**

All students share two commonalties: All love to succeed and all love to learn, but when the learning experience is laced with repeated failure, shame, discouragement, and accusation, learning is an experience to be dreaded. For the sake of one's own self-esteem, one's own self-image, the embarrassed student often distances himself or herself from the system in which he or she fails. Thus, the teacher is met with apathy and even antagonism.

If students are challenged with significant learning tasks consisting of skills relevant to their lives, however, and enter them assured that learning will not result in humiliation, then they are far more likely to pursue the task successfully. No student minds being challenged to think, but every student (every person, for that matter) very much minds being doomed to failure. To be a legend, a teacher must practice these traits praised by students. It means being patient, nonthreatening, and encouraging. This can easily be achieved when the teacher shows that he or she is willing to share the responsibility for disappointing test scores: "I should have prepared you better, maybe with more examples or a better review." The point is that the teacher encourages sincere effort because he or she does not distance himself or herself from the results, regardless of how gratifying they are.

Additionally, in the legend's classroom, it's okay to be wrong because everyone realizes the search for the correct response is far more valued than the response itself. In the legend's classroom, making an honest effort and volunteering answers—thinking—are more highly valued than embarrassment is feared. We repeat: Thinking skills are more highly valued than embarrassment is feared. In the legend's classroom, effort is what matters, what is rewarded, and what results in success.

> *In the legend's classroom, the observer will likely find the following types of behavior:*
>> *Questions are praised before being answered: "That is a very insightful question."*
>> *Wrong answers are praised before being corrected: "I know exactly how you were thinking."*
>> *Effort is as highly recognized as success: "This is the most successfully organized answer yet."*

Concern 3: Students Wish to View Their Instructors as Professionals, Models From Whom They May Learn ("motivated," "intense," "wise," and "dedicated")

The best teachers love their fields. Students might even make fun of their dedication—"Old Man Brown lives, eats, and breathes physics"—but deep inside, they admire that passion; they envy such commitment. Science teachers seem more like scientists than teachers. Vocational people are professionals in their fields, working outside the classroom as well. English people are readers and writers, and physical education department staff enjoy good health and recreation. Legends are not shams. They love their areas of expertise and communicate that love to their students daily. The legends' real reward isn't on payday, it is when their passion is caught by the students. That is a big-time return on anyone's investment.

> A gruff, older teacher of 25 years was in his room working when a young substitute came up to him, absolutely beaming. "Remember me?" she asked.
>
> Politely, he admitted that he didn't. She told him that she was a former student of his, but that didn't help: He still did not remember her.
>
> Unperturbed, she told him her name, as though revealing a secret, but he still had to say he did not remember her.
>
> Like a trooper, she was not deterred by his bad memory and admitted that she had given her married name, but her

maiden name was something else. But that didn't help either, and the older teacher could only look sorrowfully at her.

She allowed him his poor memory still, however, admitting that it was many years ago that she had been in his class. As she named several of her classmates, the older teacher had to confess he remembered them well, along with others she hadn't mentioned.

Her face darkened, and somewhere between tears and anger she said, "I took all your classes. . . . You're the reason I became a teacher!"

The point is simple: When teachers model the passion they have in their fields, they not only instruct more effectively, they also, however unintentionally, inspire.

Concern 4: Students Seem to Desire Teachers Who Are Sensitive to Their Needs and the Exigencies of Their Existence Within Which They Must Operate ("compassionate," "honest," "understanding," even-tempered," "fair," and "caring")

Over the years, we have had the opportunity to work with a number of student teachers. In every case there comes a time when the student teacher comes up to his or her supervising teacher and presents the same dilemma: "On the one hand I want to be sensitive to the kids' needs, but on the other, I don't want to be a sucker for every story they tell."

Simply put, do you wish to be popular or respected? The response to this question is not an easy one, and it presents a dilemma that most educators face at one time or another, but that doesn't make responding any easier. Perhaps the best response goes something like this: If we admit that we cannot always be perfect (Okay, we'll never be perfect), then our course of action is more evident. Given the choice, how do we chose to err? (a) Would we rather be the teacher who is never fooled because we don't give the student a break? or (b) Would we rather be the teacher who may occasionally buy into a falsehood because we prefer to believe the student and choose instead to do the right thing as though the student were indeed being truthful?

The best people are honest, compassionate, and understanding. The legend is too. Admittedly, neither choice is really desirable, and the thought of students pulling a fast one and laughing about it (and us) later is not attractive, but having to choose, the legend would rather be viewed as a sucker than a cynic.

> *When dealing with students who have failed to turn in an assignment, we would be wise to remember what it last felt like when we were pulled over for speeding by an officer of the law.*
>
> *At that moment, we did not demand justice, we craved mercy and a second chance. And when that officer finally decided to let us go with only a warning, we were forever grateful.*

Wouldn't it be nice to be viewed that way by our students? Repeat offenders are, of course, dealt with sternly and quickly, but the legend understands that students make errors in judgment and are willing to give second chances, accept the dubious excuse, and be human. At least one time.

No one is perfect; the world can't function in only black and white. One must be flexible enough in one's exercise of authority so as not to back himself or herself into a corner.

When weighed together, these four areas of concerns clearly present students' expectations for the environment in which they may most readily learn. Caring teachers are the ones who are willing to massage their own personalities in those directions. That is a neat segue to a discussion of attitudes.

PROMOTING STRONG ATTITUDES

One need not travel far into any profession before he or she hears someone say in one breath, "What potential!" and in the next breath, "But he's going nowhere with that attitude!" echoing the old saw, "Attitude is everything." What kind of an "attitude" should a teacher carry into the classroom each day? Well, it would appear that most legends share a number of attitudinal commonalties.

Looking for the Best

Effective teachers are always looking for the best in everyone. They are not confused with reports of past successes or failures as determinants of future behavior. They do not confuse an older sibling's abilities with those of a younger child. They do not bring prejudices into the class based on socioeconomics, race, gender, or any other demographic. Every child is approached as a unique and special individual, and every individual begins every day with a clean slate. These teachers enter every day believing in the efficacy of what they are about to do. More so than other teachers, legends believe that attitude, more often than not, determines success. The question of attitude is of such preeminence in education that we are willing to say this: Teachers burn out when and only when they have resigned themselves to being burned out. It is virtually a conscious choice—but so is attitude.

Taking Risks

Effective teachers are competitive risk takers. The best teachers share one important characteristic: They want to be the best—not at the expense of others, not by denigrating their peers, but in the positive pride in their own success. The legend does not fear outside audits of his or her work—he or she welcomes them as an opportunity to shine. The legend does not dread classroom observations; he or she relishes them as a time to "strut his or her stuff." The legend enjoys having others see him or her when he or she is effective. The legend realizes that at the heart of any game, including the game of teacher evaluation, is the scoreboard, and the legend is competitive enough to desire to be the MVP. Through the legend's healthy competitiveness and desire to be the best, he or she models successful behavior for students. The legend believes he or she can teach anyone anything, and students leave the room feeling the same.

Being Fair

Effective teachers are persistently fair. There are no favorites, and what soon becomes surprisingly apparent to the students is that all the rules apply to all the students all the time. Neither a student's academic success in the class nor his or her excellent behavior nor his or her extracurricular involvement earns preferential treatment from the teacher. Another way to express this very profound thought is that the teacher's attitude is not a reflection of the students' attitudes; in fact, the opposite is true. The teacher's attitude is infectious.

Appreciating the Pull and Tug of the Class

The most effective teachers do not resent the students that make them be their best. To the contrary, the opposite may be true. The legend knows that any teacher can achieve a degree of success with well-mannered, similarly valued students. These apples of education's eye could be placed in a library and 12 years later emerge with an adequate education. Great teachers are not needed by these SAT-praised wonders. It is the average achiever and the disadvantaged child who truly *need* the great teacher. It is with a great teacher that these students can most significantly make a difference. Conventional wisdom suggests that greatness is defined by adversity and the way in which it is met. Our heroes don't overcome advantages and pleasures—they overcome tragedy and personal obstacles, and regardless of whether they may actually resent those challenges, they behave as though they don't. Legends understand that actions need not always follow feelings—in fact, they may precede them. The fact that the teacher may not wish to have a particular student in class, that he or she may not wish to teach a given unit or even an entire class, does not mean the teacher has to communicate those feelings in behavior. Instead, by acting as though he or she appreciates the student, the unit, or even the class, the teacher may begin to communicate positive feelings. Legends do not resent the difficulties of their profession—they embrace them, and in doing so, overcome them. That attitude is lived daily by a school's most effective teachers.

It is not true, however, that we believe all teachers should do their undergraduate work at Pollyanna Tech and their masters program at Mary Poppins University. We can be realists about this. We have to admit that attitude is not everything, but it is an integral part of our triangular definition of the most desirable personality for successful educators. The final, and perhaps most important, aspect of the concept of attitude is that it is the most obvious to students. A poor attitude cannot be hidden for long, if at all. A good attitude, on the other hand, cannot be contained; it is contagious not just to students but to other teachers and administrators as well.

DEVELOPING GOOD HABITS

This leads us to the final segment of our triangular definition of a legend's personality: the habits of special teachers. It is possible for one to have tremendous character traits and a very positive attitude and still fail, if the third and final piece of the personality puzzle is absent. The positive attributes of both character and attitude are meaningless unless they find expression in the daily habits of the teacher.

It is only in the behavior of the teacher that the positive attitudes of the legend are manifested. To ensure that these positive attributes are evident to students, the legend goes out of his or her way to display the following habits.

- First, the master teacher makes it apparent that he or she works as hard as, if not harder than, the students to ensure their success. The legend does work done nightly, just as he or she expects the students to do.
- Second, the master teacher is professional in the manner in which he or she interacts with students. Despite the fun students may have or the work they may do, the teacher does not lose focus on the professional-client relationship that must be maintained.
- Lastly, the master teacher is punctual, professional in dress, and organized. His or her daily preparedness leaves no doubt about his or her dedication and belief in the success of all students.

All three of these habits are essential to the legend's success— without them, a teacher is nothing more than a charlatan and has no right to demand the respect or hard work of the students. Only when the teacher is always prepared, professional, and diligent may he or she ask the students to emulate him or her, and if education is not grounded firmly on emulation of the instructor, then teachers are superfluous to the process of learning.

Likewise, the best teachers don't have good and bad days, at least not many of them; instead, they have good and better days. Their dealings with students are not a reflection of their personal feelings; instead, they professionally follow through commitments to their students regardless of personal concerns or problems. They are always polite in dealing with students, and never confuse their real jobs of educating the young with the nuisance of sometimes correcting behavior.

Every day a student walks into the classroom of a legend, that student knows that he or she will be treated with respect and concern. The student knows that the teacher has prepared a meaningful educational experience; there are no "free days" in a legend's classroom. The student knows that he or she will be held up to tough standards and that he or she will have to work hard to succeed, but more important, the student knows that the teacher will be working just as hard to see that success is realized.

CONCLUSIONS

The whole in this case is greater than the sum of its parts. The legend does more than combine the traits, attitudes, and habits described. He or she is more than that total. The master teacher is outgoing; he or she is personable, exciting, energetic. The legend is dynamic, and the sheer force of his or her will makes the legend effective beyond the norm.

Are good teachers born or made? We come full circle to admit truthfully, and a bit unwillingly, that the marvelous combination of characteristics of legends are probably if not innate, then most certainly nurtured far before the legend ever applied for a job. Acknowledging this, however, we must return to the enigma we first proffered and suggest again that it would be best if we believed as if this were not so. We are better off knowing that if we try to foster these characteristics, traits, attitudes, and work habits in all our teachers, we will have a tremendously positive influence on education. In doing so, we might rediscover something that most of our mothers tried to teach us long ago—it is not necessary for our behavior to follow our emotions; instead, it is very possible for the opposite to be true and for our emotions to follow our behavior. Perhaps if we all made a greater effort at acting like the teacher we've described as the legend, then one day, we might start to feel that way as well.

2

---◆---

NOTHING SUCCEEDS
LIKE SUCCESS

Perhaps because he or she is a legend, the master teacher is suc-cessful, or perhaps because he or she has always been successful, the master teacher is a legend. Regardless of the direction in which the two influence each other, the fact remains that the master teacher is successful. It is this cyclical relationship to which this chapter is dedicated.

Even casual observations make it clear that the legend is a success because he or she experiences success, and the legend experiences success because he or she is a success. Sufficiently obtuse? Believe it or not, we don't think so, but perhaps what we really mean may appear more cogent by presenting this chapter's four main points:

- Establishing the analogy

- Developing professional pride

- Living in the loop

- Building the partnership

ESTABLISHING THE ANALOGY

There is in this chapter, and throughout the entire book, an analogy that forms the underpinnings of much of our philosophy on education as well as the notion of the legend, and that analogy involves athletic programs in the schools, or more specifically the behavior of most successful athletic coaches. We'd like to propose an examination of head coaches from an interesting and, we hope, fresh perspective. Please note: We're not concerned here with the value of sports in schools, or for that matter any of the arguments that may exist between the curricular and the co-curricular factions. Instead, what we are concerned with is the approach taken by many successful head coaches: what they do, based on what we perceive as some significant similarities to and differences from the classroom teacher's situation. We believe that an objective examination of the coach's situation when compared to the experience of the classroom teacher will reveal some germane conclusions.

We need to begin with the identification of a significant similarity as well as several important differences between the two situations.

A Significant Similarity

Coaches, like classroom teachers, deal with the same age students, and thus with the same population, the same demographics, the same home environs, and the same parents. Therefore, a coach's success or failure may be measured against the same raw material as the classroom teacher's.

Several Significant Differences

Coaches, unlike teachers, by and large are not assigned students by a master schedule, but must recruit them. The head coach is responsible for the popularity and desirability of his or her program. The coach must attract students to the program and keep their interest.

Coaches, unlike teachers, must sell their activities, not only to students but also to parents, communities, and school boards. Coaches must continually justify the considerable amounts spent on their programs, and, frequently, must spearhead efforts to raise additional funds.

Coaches, unlike teachers, are expected generally, to win—not at any cost, but at an acceptable one—in competition with other local schools. Their successes and failures are published, covered by local papers. The results of their efforts appear daily in statistical form on the sports pages.

Coaches, unlike teachers, do not have programs or positions guaranteed by state mandate or tenured by school codes. What they do face is the prospect that, tomorrow, important team members may quit or transfer to another school. What coaches must live with is the knowledge that next week the board may cut their budget or eliminate their program or that next year they may not be coaching.

Although analogical in nature, each of the descriptors above is relatively incontestable and universal, and their implications are even more so. What is implicit in these observations is clear—every head coach must be successful to keep his or her job. Our analogy, consequently, suggests that by looking at some of the common behaviors of successful head coaches, because they do deal with the same general population as teachers, we can, in fact, specify some implications for the types of behaviors that the successful teacher, a legend, will also share to make his or her classroom more successful.

Behavior 1: Recognition and Promotion

Because of the nature of the position, the head coach promotes a program vigorously from pep assemblies to posters to camps to fundraisers. All is done to make the program successful because, finally, nothing promotes a program more than recognition of its past success. If the season is not going well, the coach recognizes accomplishments by star individuals. If no individuals shine on the playing field, then the coach recognizes the fine effort being made by all. Regardless of how, the coach promotes the success of the program.

Implications for Teacher Behavior

That the legend must also recognize success in the classroom is so apparent, so significant, that we dedicate an entire chapter (Chapter 6) to methods by which success may be recognized; for now, suffice it to imagine a pep assembly for academic success, to imagine the teacher as cheerleader for his or her students' own gains, an active promoter of classroom success by filling the room with visual recognition of student achievement.

Behavior 2: Organization

This too is such an important issue that we dedicate an entire chapter (Chapter 5) to it, but briefly, it has been our experience that the most successful coaches are the most organized. Because of the limited time they have, their practices and schedules must be precisely organized, frequently down to the minute. The most successful coaches have an urgency about them during their preseason, season, and postseason. Their practices are intense; their timetables are non-negotiable.

Implications for Teacher Behavior

In contrast, the classroom teacher may seem almost relaxed, at times almost nonchalant, about the business at hand. We suggest that the legend shares the same intensity, feels and communicates the same urgency to succeed, to move on and bring the students along with him or her. To do so, the legend is organized, rehearsed, and directed—keeping the student on task and focused on the material to be learned.

Behavior 3: Goal Orientation

Upon first reading, one might argue that our analogy to sports may break down here; how can the coach's elementary fixation on 60 minutes of action whose results are tallied on a scoreboard apply to the complexities of the classroom? We refute that rejection most vehemently, however, by suggesting that the realities of the classroom, to the contrary, are far more concrete than the ambiguities of the artificial game arena.

Implications for Teacher Behavior

The legend must be even more concretely aimed at measurable goals than the athletic coach. The legend begins, like the coach, by knowing what success looks like. Because the legend's job is not to teach but rather to see that students learn, the legend has a very specific concept of how success appears. All the legend's efforts work backward from a very clear conception of what success looks like, how it will be measured for the particular area or class, and what students will be able to do following instruction. The legend does not operate from a vague generalization about "student growth"; rather, the legend works from a specific understanding of how the product of efforts should manifest itself in terms of students' abilities.

The legend is goal oriented, and such orientation make success much easier. This preoccupation with success must work at two levels.

At the first level, success (real success) must be measured at the individual plane. The movement toward authentic assessment, as opposed to the traditional end-of-the unit, forced-response test, is in the right direction. No teacher, and certainly not the legend, should accept the cramming of information into short-term memory for the test as successful learning. The legend assesses individual success at a much more instinctive level. He or she discovers if the skills, concepts, and methods of that unit have been truly internalized. He or she seeks to discover if these are now tools the students can actually use. Having studied Locke's theory of democratic principles, the student can do more than merely cite a list of those tenets, he or she can determine which aspects of modern America are Lockian in nature and which no longer are. Learning is measured at the application levels to demonstrate true understanding and grasp of material.

On a broader level, the legend is oriented to classwide success, even perhaps at the department level. Success at these levels can be measured in such diverse manners as the following:

- The percentage of students who score at the C level or above within a class
- Outside audits such as nationally normed, standardized tests, and, more commonly today, statewide minimal competency exams
- College entrance exams such as the SAT, ACT, and AP
- Grades on final examinations
- The percentage of students who succeed at the next grade level

- Outside awards in interscholastic competitions
- The number of projects satisfactorily completed
- Portfolio assessments of actual performance

The most important thing is that just like the coach, the legend measures success with the intent to use such data to redesign curriculum and remodel pedagogy.

Behavior 4: Professional Development

Coaches live to attend clinics. Given the choice, we suspect that most coaches would rather see their equipment budget cut before losing the opportunity to attend their beloved clinics. Social life at such clinics temporarily aside, the clinics are filled with successful professionals who have come to share techniques. Statisticians (in educational terms, clinicians) are not invited to speak, only successful coaches who bring their methods and philosophies to share with others. World Series managers, NFL quarterbacks, WNBA coaches, NCAA champions are presented as keynote speakers, their words coveted like manna from heaven. Coaches understand that the human element is so important that hearing what statisticians have to say about the games would not help nearly as much, would not inspire others to success. Coaches turn to models of success—not theory.

Implications for Teacher Behavior

Likewise, the legend looks toward other successful classroom teachers to find what they have done. The legend seeks perpetual development realizing that such improvement is not a destination as much as it is a journey; that one never really is a success, one merely continues becoming one. What the legend does today as the school's best teacher will be inadequate tomorrow. He or she is a legend because he or she is devoted to perpetual growth as a teacher.

Behavior 5: Flexibility

Coaches have trouble hiding their failures. Newspapers and videotapes see to that. It's hard to explain to a student body or board of education that two wins during a basketball season was a tremendous success, year after year. It is apparently much easier for classroom teachers to offer that contention. In fact, the anthem for many schools, sung to the tune of "Mine Eyes Have Seen the Glory," is "Scores Don't Tell the Whole Story."

Implications for Teacher Behavior

Successful teachers are the ones most interested in identifying their faults and remediating them, rather than devising reasons the results don't matter or even denying that the shortcomings exist. This concept is covered more thoroughly in "Living the Loop." Suffice it to say, the legend works to discover his or her own weaknesses and then works twice as diligently to address them.

Before we put this analogy to bed, we must include a realistic renunciation and acknowledgment. Neither the successful athletic program nor the successful classroom can be called successful merely by statistics. Numbers never tell the whole story, and we are all aware of how easily manipulated they may be. In the same vein, let us reiterate by stressing that our coach model seeks to win at an "acceptable cost" only. There is more to sports than just the scoreboard, and there is more to education than merely test results.

Anyone remotely involved with education recognizes that teachers are immersed with nurturing students as well as seeing that they learn. Relationships are essential to this development, and the ruthless, win-at-all-costs coach who shows no respect or care for the players, who exploits them for his own reputation, does them no service. Likewise, the teacher who exists to notch his or her belt with every 30 on the ACT regardless of the price paid by the students is a legend only in his or her own mind. We stand by our original tenet, however, that the legend is the teacher most interested in measuring students' real success and in revising efforts to make that success more common. The legend is the ultimately flexible instructor.

DEVELOPING PROFESSIONAL PRIDE

As described in Chapter 1, the legend is a complex individual with many personality traits, not the least of which is a driving competitiveness. The legend wants, simply, to be the best teacher in the school. It is professional pride. Pride, of course, is a conundrum in the Western world. Ancient Greek playwrights prejudiced us toward it by naming it hubris. Modern playwrights have furthered that prejudice by telling us that our heroes should be "humble but lovable." We think the truth, not too surprisingly, lies somewhere in the middle.

The paradox between the type of "good" pride in what one does and the type of "bad" pride that leads to downfalls is worthy of analysis. The legend desires to be and takes pride in being one of the best (if not the best) teacher in the school. Such a pride we'll call *motivational pride*. In the legend's case, motivational pride drives him or her to be better. It is the source of energy to improve. It forces the legend to examine himself or herself constantly, to find ways to be more successful. Motivational pride is almost entirely internal. It does not feed on praise from others or outside reinforcement; it satisfies itself by recognizing that, finally, only internal acceptance truly matters.

This motivational pride manifests itself in some very observable, concrete behaviors and attitudes, all of which legends share.

Motivational Pride Drives the Teacher to Acknowledge the Efficacy of the Educational Process

The legend recognizes that he or she is a part of what's going on holistically and that the success of students is a direct reflection on the teacher. Motivational pride does not let the teacher distance himself or herself from how well the students do; consequently, the teacher is driven through this good pride to become a more effective instructor to the students, while still encouraging and helping students in their other school endeavors.

Motivational Pride Helps the Teacher Make Choices, Because It Demands That the Teacher's Highest Priority Is the Success of the Students

Wanting to be the best easily lets the teacher look toward others to find ways to improve. The legend becomes adept at borrowing techniques and strategies from other teachers. For example, the lab exam format from anatomy suddenly becomes a new way to test poetry without running off 30 copies of 10 poems for all students. Now the students simply rotate from station to station. The vocational director borrows a reading strategy from the English department to help the students learn more from independent reading. Master teachers borrow from each other on a daily basis.

Motivational Pride Keeps the Teacher
Working Throughout the Evening to Get
the Lessons Done and the Papers Scored

The teacher is able to spend long hours at home scoring and preparing. We must admit, however, that unlike any other profession, education rests on the rather ridiculous premise that teachers do $1/3$ to $1/2$ of their work at home—without reimbursement. Nonetheless, this motivational pride gets the teacher through trying times and more important helps the teacher smile when some uninformed third party who never has worked 6 16-hour days in a row smiles and says, "Well, at least you get 3 months vacation every year."

The legend is not a hypocrite by demanding that all student work be turned in on time while holding papers and tests for several weeks before scoring them.

Motivational Pride Demands That
the Teacher be Absolutely Honest in
Dealing With Students and Other Teachers

Such honesty, not only with the students but also with other teachers is what makes motivational pride an acceptable characteristic. While the teacher is in competition with other teachers to be the best, motivational pride forces the teacher to deal openly and cooperatively with peers. One would not want to be the best because of efforts meant to subvert others' successes. What works is shared. Motivational pride works schoolwide, and the sense of team permeates all interactions among teachers.

Motivational Pride Makes
the Teacher a Risk Taker

Taking risks means constant manipulation of surroundings, curricula, and pedagogy to keep the competitive edge and to work toward greater success continually. When this competitive edge, the main product of motivational pride, is gone, then so too is the reason for working. Michael Jordan understood this when he walked away from basketball for a short period of time, feeling he had done everything there was to do. To be a legend means to be working toward perfection—not attaining it.

Motivational pride is most visibly manifested in our efforts to see the students succeed. It is what takes us above and beyond the call, even of education. It is the promise we made at our interviews; it is the tacit promise we make to every student: to take the student as far as we can. Are such promises, explicit or implicit, to be belied by other motives or behavior later? We think not. The legend is professionally proud and is in a healthy competition with peers to be the best in the school—more important, to be the best he or she can be.

On the other hand, the bad type of pride we call *debilitating pride* is a destructive characteristic. Debilitating pride is egotistical and competitive at a cut-throat level. It is never concerned about the entire school environment, nor even about the students, operating instead only at the individual level. Its origin is in the insecurity of the individual. It is derisive and dividing. At its best, debilitating pride drives the teacher to guard his or her techniques carefully, never sharing them. At its worst, it is mean-spirited and targets others critically as a way to make itself look better. It drives students into critical opinions of others and builds cliques among faculties.

Some Important Conclusions

In an age where the politically correct "C" word is cooperation, we propose that the other "C" word, competition, is not totally malevolent. In fact, when driven by motivational pride as we've defined it, competition within a staff should most likely be viewed as pretty healthy. The best teams anywhere are those where healthy competition exists for starting positions. Every baseball aficionado understands that to have an effective number three hitter requires a great clean-up hitter, and likewise the clean-up hitter is only as good as the number five batter. Motivational pride suggests the same kind of healthy, competitive teamwork, each individual proudly working to be the best while enjoying the success of the entire team.

LIVING IN THE LOOP

"Living in the loop" is a concept foreshadowed frequently in this chapter and one that reappears throughout the book. (So this better be pretty darn good. We think it is, and that's good pride.) The legend is most probably the most flexible teacher on a staff, for the legend understands the fluidity of the educational process. Each year, different students arrive with different needs, different backgrounds, and different chemistries. What succeeded last year will not necessarily succeed this year or next year. What needs to be taught changes. The way it is to be taught needs to change. As the legend grows, so does his or her pedagogical preference; his or her style changes in response to the varying needs and student chemistries of the classes.

As a result of this constant state of flux, the legend soon learns that to be successful means to live in a loop. For the legend, education is a perpetual loop made up of several distinct steps: planning, executing, debriefing, replanning, and so on. Each step is interdependent on the others, and each is equally necessary to the existence of the entire loop.

Planning

Step 1

The loop begins with careful planning. Because the legend wishes to be successful and knows that, by and large, success is determined by measurable data, then planning begins with the identification of the set of skills students must master by the time of the measurement. This identification of goals is followed immediately by division of those goals or skills into sequenced learning units divided into a manageable pacing chart, one coordinated with the district's testing and grading policies as well as its schedules. Generation of a curriculum by any means other than backward from desired outcomes is inferior. Curriculum without goals is not curriculum; it is just subject matter.

Step 2

Once the goals that will be measured have been identified, then the legend proceeds to determine what instructional techniques in each of the units will be used, how student progress will be monitored and evaluated, what remediation techniques will be used for those failing to demonstrate proficiency of the material after the initial instruction, and what enrichment activities are available for those who master the material initially. These plans (not to be confused with the arrow-laden "lesson plans" of previous times, plans that were nothing more than an agenda of teacher behavior) remain flexible as the legend alters them as necessary as he or she works through the set of units that are, in fact, the accumulated goals of the course.

Step 3

Planning sets as its first priority mastery of the identified goals by the students. As a second priority, it aims at variety, challenge, fun, and constant reinforcement of previously mastered goals. It is always focused and always flexible, keeping in mind that the entire set of outcomes must be mastered by the time of the final measurement: hence, the intensity that drives so much of the class.

Executing

Step 1

As the legend executes the plans, he or she does so with an eye more on student learning than on teacher performance. The orientation of every class period must be on mastery of the material, not its presentation. Lectures, projects, writing assignments, worksheets, and group work are all evaluated only as they serve to help the student master the identified goals.

Step 2

Similarly, the orientation of every class period must be on the mastery of the material, not on the evaluation of student progress.

The purpose of the class is neither to separate the students by ability nor to generate grades. Evaluation of student progress should be done only after it is apparent that the students have begun to master the material. Initial learning should not be evaluated. We feel that one of the major flaws of education lies in the dictate to generate grades on every learning experience. Although acquiescing to the concept of generating scores (to avoid a lengthy argument about the philosophy behind an ungraded school system), we assert that most classroom grades are not as much a picture of how well each student has mastered a goal but how quickly. By the time of the terminal evaluation, many slower learners have such poor grades already that scoring an A is no longer possible. Instead, the concept of quick learning has become more important to American schools than thorough mastery. As the legend executes his or her plans, he or she makes certain to separate learning and mastery from assessment. Each requires its own strategies and each must remain independent to validate the essence of both.

Debriefing

Step 1

The first two steps in the loop are far from revolutionary. Okay, they're downright obvious! Almost all teachers follow them to some degree. It is this third step where the legend separates himself or herself from others. Following instruction and after measurement of students' mastery of the course's goals, the legend spends a great deal of time analyzing results. This analysis is done immediately following evaluation. It is a lengthy debriefing period during which time the legend notes what worked exceptionally well and what didn't; which goals were met and which were not.

Step 2

Detailed notes are made about the evaluation of the work. One of the best places to make these notes is on the answer key to the final measurement. By writing notes on the test itself, the instructor may be sure he or she is recording important ideas (Why make the same mistakes next year?) and forcing himself or herself to redesign the measurement the following term, not allowing himself or herself to pull some tired test from a file and run it off year after year after year.

Step 3

Where there was success, the legend wants to be sure that the same procedure can be followed again. The legend is very concerned about identification of what worked. Success should no more be the product of chance than failure. Notes can be in both statistical and anecdotal form, but they should be made as closely to the assessment as possible, while ideas remain fresh. The legend seeks to identify not only the success of the course but also the explanation for that success. This analysis is carefully noted for the next year's instructional period of the same outcomes.

Step 4

As suggested earlier, no teacher on the staff craves feedback as much as the legend, and this does not mean just feedback about what succeeded. The legend wants to identify areas of failure as well. In debriefing, the legend identifies goals not met and determines why failure occurred. It was our earlier precept that the legend believes in the efficacy of education and shares both success and failure with students. This debriefing is not an exercise in creating excuses for failure. Those excuses don't need a legend, they don't even need a teacher. Excuses for failure permeate our society; students bring them to class in the form of low expectations. Instead, the legend determines how failures may be lessened or even turned into successes the next time. Rather than bemoaning what students can't do, the legend prepares to compensate for what the family, the community, or society have not provided for the student.

Replanning

Step 1

Finally, there is the replanning. This is the step that completes the loop, and the legend is right back where he or she started. Having identified success, the causes for that success are made a part of the next term's strategies. Having also identified failures, the legend redesigns that section of instruction to lessen the incidence of failure and increase the success. It is in the latter that the legend must be the most creative, the most flexible.

Step 2

Factors outside of the legend's control are totally ignored. Because we cannot lower the divorce rate of our children's parents or raise those parents' socioeconomic levels or increase the educational level of their mothers, these issues are discounted. Those factors that the legend can control (and because he or she believes in the efficacy of education, perforce, these must be the important ones), the legend redesigns.

Step 3

In a related matter, the legend has no qualms about taking problems to others for their suggestions, or even to groups of peers. The legend's ego is subservient to his or her competitive nature to succeed. The legend realizes it is ridiculous to ask students to try to do their best if the legend is unwilling to follow that same advice. So the legend replans under the belief that his or her efforts can result in improved learning for all students.

Step 4

In a final consideration, the legend keeps this rule of thumb in mind as he or she is replanning units: For every item added, one item must be deleted. Time is of such essence to the teacher that adding and adding material will eventually become counterproductive. The legend is just as prepared to remove material or activities as he or she is to add.

BUILDING THE PARTNERSHIP

The final aspect of success involving the legend is probably the most important. Simply put: Success breeds credibility and therefore trust. By being successful with students, the legend engenders more success. There is in every school that teacher for whom the students do the work. It might be the only class for which they do homework, but they do it for that one teacher. This teacher is the one who somehow gets everything done in a timely fashion, including completing forms for the central office. The concept that success engenders success is probably best exemplified in a story from the lore of professional baseball.

> In what is probably nothing more than an apocryphal tale, the great Ted Williams was batting late in a close game with runners on first and second and no outs. Williams had worked the count full to 3 and 2. There was a second-year pitcher on the mound and a rookie catcher behind the plate. After shaking off several signs, the pitcher came set. He rocked back and fired a low inside fast ball that Williams took.
>
> "Ball four," called the umpire, sending Williams to first and moving the lead runner over to third.
>
> "Ball!" challenged the rookie catcher as he rose, turned, and took off his mask. "You have got to be kidding me! How can you call that a ball?"
>
> The older ump, unruffled by the youngster's passion, slowly removed his mask and explained calmly to the rookie, "Son, I know that was a ball, because if that had been a strike, Mr. Williams would have hit it."

The same is true for the legend in the classroom. The legend's reputation precedes him or her. Although the legend may be regarded as the toughest grader in the school as well as the most demanding instructor, the legend's classes are popular, and not without reason. As the legend has more and more students succeed, both in the class he or she teaches and in classes students later take, the more the legend's credibility grows and the more students and parents become attuned to trusting the legend's judgment and doing what is asked of them. People believe in the legend, so both the teacher and students succeed more frequently.

We have come full circle from the chapter's start—the legend is a success because he or she has been successful, thus increasing the likelihood of future success as well.

Every victory the legend enjoys decreases the resistance he or she is likely to find in the classroom or community. When the legend's records point toward widespread success, students and parents "buy into" the program. With growing trust is the increased likelihood of completed assignments, sincere efforts to succeed, and seeking extra help when problems arise. These characteristics are the biggest reason for increased success. As the legend grows, parents begin to help, sometimes even unknowingly, by denying excuses at home, assisting with homework, demanding success. The legend's reputation has solved problems before they arise.

On a very simple level, the legend is the teacher who can tell the students to jump and be met with a round of "how high." Back to our original analogy about athletics: Students put themselves through nightly physical torment because they believe such agony will help them be victorious on the playing field the next weekend. Imagine how hard students would work if they could be made to believe that school work would benefit them. They need not like the legend (but probably do); however, they must trust the legend!

Students believe the legend knows his or her business and that he or she is acting in their best interest. Those two beliefs are the stuff of legends. They are what makes the legend so much more successful than any other teacher. When these two beliefs exist in the students and their parents, then the real partnership for educational success has been built. Such a partnership between caring parents and respected teachers may sometimes even be built at the schoolwide level, but more important for everyone reading this book, it can always be cultivated at the individual teacher's level.

A TOUCH OF REALITY

One final word on failures: The reader may have sensed a rather hopeless idealism on the part of the authors (to which we reply that we all know that only hopeless romantics become teachers anyway, so why the sudden interest in realism?). We confess to a degree of idealism, having found that to be a far better vehicle than pessimism or nihilism, but we are not totally oblivious to the real world either.

The legend doesn't reach everyone.
Not everyone can be reached.

In the final analysis, students retain the rights of the individual, including the right to self-determination and the right to fail.

The legend believes he or she can shape people, and he or she takes pride in the product: caring, self-assured, intellectual young dults. But that pride and that idealism do not negate the concepts discussed in the next chapter about standards and expectations. The legend enables more students to achieve and to succeed, even if he or she is unable to enable everyone to succeed, and the verbs are what are important in this thought. Good teachers don't make students succeed, but enable them to through motivation, planning, and pedagogy. The legend enables more than most, but not all. He or she doesn't necessarily accept these defeats gracefully, but they are accepted. No other teacher is so personally involved and responsible for students' success. No other teacher hurts so poignantly when he or she and the students fail, but, realistically and unfortunately, the legend has failures too—just not as many, and certainly not as casually, as other teachers.

CONCLUSIONS

We end where we began (a little rhetorical legerdemain): The legend is a success because he or she experiences success, and the legend experiences success because he or she is a success. Through pride and through competitiveness, the legend forces himself or herself to exist in a loop of planning and replanning. The driving force through all the legend does is students' success. We have chosen to call the master teacher a legend because his or her success is predicated on the trust placed by students and parents alike. Over many years, the master teacher has earned a legendary role in the school. Parents hope their children will have this teacher; they express those wishes frequently. The legend's status gains him or her more student and parent cooperation, which in turn makes the legend a far more successful teacher.

3

ESTABLISHING
HIGH EXPECTATIONS

There are those who argue that the successful teacher ought to be more concerned with the affective side of students rather than with the growth of cognitive skills. To a degree, this attitude may be correct, but to a larger degree, it is not. Bedside manner is often touted as being very important to a doctor's success. But how many patients choose the doctor with a more pleasant bedside manner over a doctor with a higher patient survival rate?

Likewise, when a parent sends children to school, it is not so that they may make more adult friends, but so that they may acquire those cognitive skills necessary to succeed later in education and consequently in life. Those parents expect the teachers' primary focus to be the development of cognitive skills. Of course, they do not wish for their children's teachers to be insensitive or disagreeable, but they do want them focused on learning as the primary function of the school experience.

No area of discussion concerning the master teacher, the legend, could possibly elicit as much disagreement as the area of expectations and standards. Among teachers themselves is a wide range of beliefs concerning this issue. The beginning teacher may feel there is a tremendous void in existing guidelines by which to shape professional expectations, unless, by default, we allow our textbooks to shape not only our curriculum but also our expectations. Neither is a sound option. To explore the area of expectations, we must look at the following issues:

- Determining expectations
- Identifying the pitfalls
- Communicating expectations
- Maintaining consistency and objectivity
- Removing the excuses

DETERMINING EXPECTATIONS

When we arrive at our first teaching assignment, our expectations for our students are characteristically very high. We often try to begin by teaching the students in our care that which we have just learned, not at all remembering where we were intellectually a few years earlier. As a result, although some of our students do rise to these high expectations, a great number do not. For this reason more than any other, our first experience with teaching secondary students may indeed be quite disappointing. Students can't seem to grasp simple concepts (as we did during our senior year in college); their work ethic seems nonexistent (unlike the hours we just spent finishing our final papers); and they show no foresight into their futures at all (in great contrast to us, because we just finished our first job search). Our disappointment swells to the point that we begin to wonder if we've made the right career choice.

In reality, the problem is that most of us entered the teaching field without a firm set of expectations of what kind of work the students should do, what we could expect them to grasp, or even what kind of effort we ought to expect of them in and out of class. The first obstacle to becoming a legend, in short, is setting appropriate expectations and standards for students.

How then does a teacher begin to formulate realistic expectations for students' work and reasonable standards by which he or she will evaluate progress? Luckily, there is a very definite series of steps the teacher may take to begin to formulate both expectations and standards.

Creating the Vision

It is impossible to set realistic expectations for students if the teacher does not begin with a vision of what the end product will be. The legend makes certain to start with such a vision: a set of realistic expectations of the skills and knowledge the students will have mastered by the end of instruction. The vision may be formed through the investigation of several sources of information:

- Standardized, nationally normed exams
- Standards that may exist within a state
- Existing district information
- Experienced teachers and administration

Standardized, Nationally Normed Exams

A strong point of origin for the setting of any teacher's expectations is existing, nationally normed examinations. Tests such as the ACT PLAN, the PSAT, the ACT, the SAT, and all the advanced placement examinations, as well as the many commercially available standardized achievement tests, are predicated on the simple belief that at a stipulated point in education, there exists a body of skills and knowledge that students will have mastered. It is only logical, therefore, to begin by determining these expectations and working backward from them.

A teacher of 11th-grade U.S. history, uncertain what to teach as he covers the nation's time line, begins to formulate expectations for his students by examining the U.S. history AP exam. That exam indicates that by the time students take the test, they are expected to contrast traditional views of World War II with revisionist views of the war in a cogent essay.

Now the teacher knows that in addition to merely covering World War II, he must do so in a fashion that will teach his students the concept of traditional views as opposed to revisionist perspectives, as well as develop in students the ability to express their ideas articulately in written form. The expectations have been set.

Likewise, the more often a teacher finds the same expectations present throughout a wide range of different tests, then the more he or she can be assured that those truly are valid expectations to hold for students.

Standards That May Exist Within a State

In many states today, the movement toward objective-based curricula has resulted in the publication of a series of academic goals for all youngsters, K-12, in all areas of studies. In such a situation, the teacher need only consult the state's learner outcomes to formulate realistic expectations.

> In Illinois, the state's goals for education identify five outcomes in the area of language arts, one of which is students must be able to interpret and evaluate a variety of written material. The goals suggest that by grade 10, this would include the ability to recognize fallacies of logic.
>
> Because this expectation already exists, it becomes incumbent on English teachers to include these goals in their design of lessons and their preparation of students. It is no longer a matter for debate—by the end of 10th grade, students should have been exposed to critical thinking skills, including Aristotelian fallacies of logic. The expectations have been set.

Existing District Information

Most districts maintain copious longitudinal files concerning student progress based on years of standardized testing. In addition, many districts regularly update carefully articulated demographic profiles of their clientele. Finally, many schools keep longitudinal results of local assessments. All these provide a broad base of information from which the investigative teacher will be able to generate reasonable expectations to meet the needs of students.

> By studying the past 10 years of scores from the Stanford Achievement Tests, a teacher may be able to identify recurring

weaknesses or strengths within a field, either of which may be used to establish more reasonable expectations for students.

Once again, the point of emphasis in creating a vision by which to set expectations and standards is to begin with an informed perspective of the students.

Experienced Teachers and Administration

Entering any new situation, the wise teacher (novice or experienced) needs to touch base with his or her peer group and administration to discover existing expectations. A department head may be amenable to passing on expectations to the teacher. Likewise, the teacher may have been hired by an administration that has specific expectations in mind. In either case, it is wise for the teacher to become cognizant of these and set goals accordingly, not, initially at least, acting as the maverick.

A final note about sources of information. Consulting experienced teachers and administrators is perhaps the best method the novice teacher has for setting reasonable standards for the evaluation of student work. Because evaluation of student work is an integral and often problematic part of any instructor's job, most teachers are forced early in their careers to arrive at some philosophical approach to grading, one with which they can live. Collegial discussions are a primary method by which one can arrive at and occasionally check one's own standards of evaluation.

Assessing Students—You Are Here!

The next step, once the teacher is comfortable with a vision of where the students need to be by the end of instruction, is to determine where the students are now. It makes little sense to design a curriculum aimed at the mastery of skills that students already possess. Similarly, it makes even less sense to design a curriculum aimed at the mastery of skills for which students lack sufficient prerequisite talents or knowledge to accomplish. The legend desires above all else at this stage to find out where the students are intellectually. This too is possible by investigating a number of venues.

Examination of Existing Data

To a degree, this has already been accomplished with the setting of expectations. As the teacher researches district information, at the same time interviewing peers and administrators, he or she most likely will be able to create a fairly accurate profile of student ability.

Pretests

Although administering pretests is a practice that finds itself more out of favor than in favor in the educational community, it nonetheless remains a valuable tool for the individual teacher to determine the actual abilities of students prior to instruction. Knowing that students are expected to be able to identify symbols, metaphors, and extended metaphors in a work of poetry by the end of the term does not mean the teacher need spend equal time on all three. Instead, the teacher may begin by giving an ungraded activity by which he or she will determine how many if any of the students have already mastered these skills. The teacher may pass out a poem and ask students to write or discuss the presence of all three in the work. Analysis of answers may well reveal that students are unable to differentiate between symbols and metaphors but fully grasp the concept of the extended metaphor. Hence, the teacher knows where instruction needs to be directed.

Pretests exist analogously to a doctor's examination. When the ailing patient enters the examination room, the expectations are crystal clear—the doctor wants the patient to be cured—but prior to prescribing any course of action, any medications, the doctor carefully identifies symptoms, determining, as nearly as he or she can, what needs to be remedied. Then, and only then, is the doctor ready to prescribe a regimen that will effect a cure.

Administering pretests or similar skill-assessing activities allow the teacher to act in the same informed fashion.

Informal Class Interaction

Something as structured as a pretest or even a practice exercise may not always be necessary. Sometimes class discussions, simple surveys, and other informal interactions may serve sufficiently well for the teacher to determine where the students are in terms of skills and knowledge mastery. Like the doctor who seeks to understand the patient beyond a mere list of symptoms, so too does the legend rely on informal methods of gathering data to create a fuller picture of students, an understanding of their world, their backgrounds, their hopes, and their expectations. All these go into the picture of knowing where the students are.

Designing the Plan

The next step, once the teacher is comfortable with a vision of where the students need to be by the end of instruction and an assessment of where the students are presently, is to work backward from the end vision to the students' present level of mastery so as to determine a pacing chart that will permit the students to progress toward that vision within the allotted time. More simply stated: The legend now knows where students are—he or she has determined where they need to be and develops the most practical plan of taking them from point A to point B.

The legend begins to fulfill the vision by determining the pedagogy most appropriate for achieving the tasks he or she has set forth. The legend continues the plan by determining a pacing chart that will guide him or her through instruction, always cognizant of the expectations that constitute the vision and the position of the students as they progress toward those expectations.

It is at this point that the teacher is able to draw on his or her training and experience to fashion the most meaningful educational experience for students, all within the framework of working from point A to point B.

Remaining Flexible

The final step in setting standards and expectations is flexibility. Flexibility for the legend is evinced in three significant arenas.

Pacing Flexibility

Once expectations are set and instruction has begun, the students are assessed regularly and the progress from point A to point B is continually monitored. These regular assessments are used in a recurring reassessment of the pacing chart and lesson plans.

> Having determined that the class needs to learn all 206 bones in the human body prior to moving on to a study of the body's tissues, the teacher has allotted 3 days of activities for mastery of this knowledge. But if the teacher finds that after 3 days most students still have not mastered the material, it is ridiculous to say that the allotted days are up and we must move on. Likewise, if the students master the material in 1 day, it is even sillier to return to it on the second and third days.

The legend's schedule is flexible, responsive to student growth as it occurs within progress toward realizing the vision.

Strategy Flexibility

Both within a single year and through several years, the legend is flexible and not married to any one activity or approach. When something doesn't work, the legend replaces it. Admitting shortcomings is not failure—ignoring them is (an original aphorism!).

Longitudinal Flexibility

The legend keeps track of students' progress, not only during the year of instruction but in future years, to make sure that the original vision was accurate and the plan was efficient. When evidence suggests otherwise, the teacher makes appropriate adjustments. The legend is flexible.

Acknowledging the Backbone

Finally, the legend is flexible but not wishy-washy. Pitfalls await every instructor as he or she sets expectations and determines standards. These potential pitfalls are discussed next, but let it suffice now to suggest that although responsive to feedback and continuing assessment of student growth, the legend does not let self-doubt worm its way into his or her thinking. Such doubt opens the door to outside pressures and cynicism, both of which undermine the process of expectation and standard setting.

Although flexible, the legend remains faithful to his or her vision. The legend finds inner peace in the full knowledge that he or she is doing the very best possible for students. The legend stands tall and believes in himself or herself. Knowing that his or her standards and expectations are in the best interest of the students, the legend remains faithful to them and is able to open many doors. This attitude is probably most succinctly exemplified in the following incident.

Several years ago, at a medallist baseball clinic in Chicago, Sparky Anderson (then manager in Cincinnati) was the keynote speaker. After his address, he took questions from the audience. One college coach rose and asked, "Sparky, what do you think is the better way to teach catchers how to throw to second on a stolen-base attempt? The direct throw sometimes sails, ending up in center field, but the one-hop throw is a little slower, and the runner . . ."

Sparky cut him off with his answer. Shaking his head, Sparky simply replied, "Doesn't matter."

The coach was obviously a little put off by the response from the manager of the world-champion Reds. "How can it not matter?"

"Either way is fine," Sparky smiled. "What matters is not the method you teach, but that you convince your team that you believe it's the method that will work. Once you convince them of that—it will."

A final word (and major caution) about expectations and standards: Our general feeling is that students will learn what is asked of them and will rise to the level of expectations. Most teachers expect way too little of their students and reward far too low levels of performance. We find this is true in almost all classes, from honors to remedial. The following experience is pretty universal.

Just out of college, in his first year of teaching, a middle school teacher decided to stress a great number of map skills. Besides the usual—find the equator, name the continents, and so on—he also made his students determine time zones and find ships lost at sea by their last known coordinates. Not to his surprise, the children did pretty well on the whole unit.

Several years later, the same teacher was looking through old materials and when he came upon that first test he had given, he was surprised to find that many of the difficult tasks that he had originally required of his students had been abandoned. Over the years, his expectations had been lowered to a far more readily achieved comfort zone.

It was at that moment that the middle school teacher first understood that the laws of atrophy apply to education just as they do to every other force in the universe. It was his first glimpse into the erosion of expectations.

Whether it is compassionate caring for self-esteem or merely the rationalization of tired teachers, there is a constant erosion of expectations and standards. As a result, it is an unfortunate reality that many of our students go woefully unchallenged throughout their education. Our overall impression of education in America is that much more can and should be demanded of our students. Our experience has repeatedly demonstrated that students will rise to our expectations and will achieve at our designated levels of success.

IDENTIFYING PITFALLS

Now that we have discussed how teachers may go about determining reasonable expectations for their students and realistic standards, there arises another task we must deal with that involves the erosion of both expectations and standards. Most teachers appear eager to sing in harmony the woeful tale of how we need to demand so much more from our students, but few seem able to rise to the occasion. Why?

The answer most certainly lies in the same place as the explanation of the natural atrophy of expectations described in the example of the middle school teacher who was surprised to find how far his expectations had fallen. This apparently naturally occurring atrophy of expectations as well as the paradox of wanting to require more and better work but somehow being unable to may be understood by looking at the forces that work against higher expectations and more stringent standards.

These forces introduce themselves to teachers in the guise of would-be partners: groups and individuals more than willing to help the teacher set and reassess expectations. Yet each presents a potential pitfall, an obstacle not only to setting high expectations and standards but also to maintaining them.

Pitfall 1: Students

The teacher's first would-be partner in the area of setting standards and expectations is an unrelenting one, yet is also the first major potential pitfall, students themselves. The teacher will face wave after wave of assertions from every class that his or her expectations are too high and standards too rigid. Students, both good and bad, both despised and favored, will as naturally bemoan what is expected of them as they will wear blue jeans and Nikes. They will initially, as if by oath, oppose any new teacher's set of standards. They will whine; they will unfavorably compare the teacher to other favored teachers; they will present and misrepresent their parents' sentiments. They may, for the first time in their lives, do elective research in the library just to find proof that expectations for them are unrealistically too high. Each new class, each new student, brings attempts to lower the teacher's standards and a fervent hope to compromise the teacher's expectations.

The Solution

This is a natural occurrence. Just as night follows day, students try to get out of as much work as possible. We will not begrudge them that. Neither will we pander to it.

This pitfall is easily avoided if one is prepared to encounter it. Whereas the good teacher is certainly sympathetic to students' concerns, willing to acknowledge the students' other commitments and priorities (and willing at times to be flexible in regard to them), the good teacher negotiates neither expectations nor standards with the students. *Students are our clients; they are not our peers.* They have no criteria of their own on which to decide what they should do or how well they should do it.

This discussion of the first potential pitfall in the setting of expectations needs to be tempered with two cautions. On one hand, we do not mean to give the teacher carte blanche to ignore the feelings and aspirations of students; rather, we suggest that the feelings and aspirations of the students do not determine expectations. Additionally, we bring back our caution about flexibility; we caution against a rigidity that does not allow for gaps in previous knowledge. If we all agree that 10th-grade students should be able to write unified, cohesive essays but we find our students don't know how to generate paragraphs, then we are surely wrong to continue with our plans without first covering the prerequisite knowledge.

The point is to develop a balance between expectations for student achievement and compassionate appreciation for student difficulties. Without this balance, the teacher is doomed. If the teacher is forever too stringent in expectation, uncaring of student concerns, then he or she alienates those students with whom he or she had a chance to succeed. If the teacher is too compassionate to student concerns, eventually expectations erode to the point of insignificance. It is a delicate and challenging balance to maintain.

Pitfall 2: Parents

The second would-be partner (and thus the second potential pitfall) to the process of setting expectations includes the parents and guardians of students (referred to simply as "parents"). Parents seem to fall into two categories: parental type 1—the "give 'em hell, Harry!" type—and parental type 2—the "have you no heart?" type.

Parent Type 1

This group thinks teachers are too soft. Members of this group believe all children, including their own, are inherently lazy and not to be trusted. They feel that teachers waste too much time on touchy-feely "stuff" and would rather we'd stick to the three Rs and "whip" the kids into shape. They're usually too busy to be involved with their children's education and expect teachers to take care of any problems that arise.

Parent Type 2

This group's interaction with teachers is always in the role of protector of the children. Members attempt to place themselves between the evil teachers and the innocent children, whom they see as having been tied to the railroad track with the train bearing down on them, forever vulnerable and forever wronged. They agree with their children that our standards are too high. They defend their children's level of success by blaming the teacher. They run for school boards often.

(Lest we vilify anyone, because this is mostly tongue in cheek, we do recognize that both types of parents act out of love and compassion for their children, trying to do what is best for them. Their motives are not to be questioned.)

The Solution

As meaningful extensions of our clients, parents deserve the opportunity to have their concerns expressed, and teachers most certainly do have an accountability to parents, but in reality, parents generally are not trained to be part of the process by which standards and expectations are determined. Through the school board members, parents' views may find voice. Although their advice and participation is always welcomed, in the final analysis, parents do not make good counsel for the setting of standards and expectations for two reasons. First, because their children are in the affected class, there is an inherent conflict of interest in their having any say about standards and expectations. Second, they are laypeople and not professionals who have studied the issues of standards and expectations. Their views tend toward the uninformed.

Experience will affirm that most contact with parents is initiated by the parent after a problem has arisen, and most parents today enter into the interchange firmly convinced that the fault lies in the teachers. Their concerns are almost universally in the external measurements of success (i.e., grades) and its ramifications (e.g., honor rolls, class ranks, car insurance deductions), not in helping their own children reach their full educational potential. Despite their care and love, parents are not a source to which we should turn to set standards and expectations.

(Special note: We present our views on what we see should be the parents' roles in setting expectations and standards both as educators [for a total of 50 years] and as parents [for a total of 43 years!]. We've sat on both sides of the table at parent-teacher conferences and recognize on which side we act professionally and rationally and on which side we act instinctively and emotionally. We do not mean to condemn parents who are involved in education; we do mean to suggest that parents, as a group, have an agenda that should preclude them from being active partners in setting expectations and standards.)

Pitfall 3: School Administration

A third logical source to which a teacher might turn for assistance in setting expectations is the administration of the district in which he or she teaches. Generalizing about all administrations is not quite as simple as it is with students and parents, but perhaps if we look at two extremes of administrative styles, we can see how administrations that tend toward the latter style pose a serious potential pitfall for the teacher looking for direction in establishing expectations.

At one extreme, we have the strong educationally oriented administration, one that has in place a system that is curriculum oriented, published, actively used by all teachers, measured, and centered around such practices as mentoring and professional collegiality. Under such an administration, the communication of standards and expectations is naturally accomplished for every teacher. Expectations are at the heart of the curriculum, the essence of measurement, and the source for pedagogical and curricular revision. In such situations, the teacher is not left afloat trying desperately to find any bit of land on which to set expectations; instead, he or she has an immediate, perpetual, and professional source for standards and expectations. This is the lucky teacher indeed.

At the other extreme is the weak, politically oriented administration that has nothing more than a knee-jerk reaction to whoever spoke most loudly at the last public meeting. In a district like this, practices are not research based, and, in fact, no real educational concerns, directions, or expectations may be communicated. The administration is certainly not to be considered a source for expectations; the teacher may have to be political himself or herself (or at least take tact to new heights) in defense of what the students really need. This is an unfortunate teacher, to be sure.

The Solution

Under the strong administration, overt direction is given to a published, skills-based curriculum and both internal and external measures by which accountability is maintained are identified. In such a case, the administration is a marvelous and accurate source of expectations. Yet under the weak administration, we find nothing more than a total disavowal of any curricular concerns and no more consideration of expectations than some weak accounting of teachers' grades and occasional pressure to pass more students, fail more students, or balance the grades more closely to some dangerous curve. The more closely an administration resembles this one, then the more the teacher is on his or her own to establish standards and expectations.

Pitfall 4: Peers

A final potential pitfall as the teacher seeks assistance in setting standards and expectations can be found, sadly, among the teacher's own peers. Sea level is the paradigm of mediocrity, and it is the physical nature of everything at rest to be drawn down toward it. Such is also the case with a great many of our peers (sorry to disappoint all the teachers who thought this section would conclude with some good, old-fashioned administration bashing). When one turns to one's peers for guidance, and one must eventually turn to one's peers, then one must be prepared to encounter three divisions of responses: good advice from another caring professional; bad advice from another caring professional; and bad advice from a tired cynic. We dearly hope (and believe) that most of the new teacher's interactions with established peers will be of the first variety. Yet we would be remiss not to warn of the second two types.

Type 1: Good Advice

This category, without doubt, encompasses the vast majority of our peers. Colleagues should be considered, and almost always are, the best source for advice concerning setting standards and expectations. The first obligation in any collegial interchange should be a comparison of standards and expectations. It is important that homogeneity of both is maintained throughout a department and, perhaps, even a school. For the beginning and experienced teacher alike, and certainly for the legend, the best source of information to help set standards and expectations is colleagues.

Type 2: Bad Advice

The second category of peers is a bit more awkward to deal with. Often, bad advice is given in the guise of loving care for students. Simply put, some experienced teachers are worn down by years of pressure and have come to believe that by expecting less of students, we are being more kind. Obviously, little in education could be farther from the truth. No service is done to the student by allowing him or her to matriculate through school without the necessary skills to succeed. The educator's job is to see that students master a basic array of skills and internalize a basic set of information. No other consideration can be allowed a higher priority, regardless of how well-meaning or compassionate the teacher may be. The students must learn: This is the credo of the legend. Advice from this group concerning the question of setting standards and expectations must be taken with that proverbial grain of salt, or perhaps the whole shaker.

Type 3: Cynical Advice

More dangerous is the third category of teacher a novice may turn to for help in setting standards and expectations. This includes teachers suffering from what is commonly referred to as "teacher burnout." We all know them. They are tired, and they are bitter. They find youthful optimism annoying. They no longer subscribe to the belief that education can make a difference in children's lives, and find anyone else's willingness to work on behalf of students preposterous. They will counsel us toward ineffectiveness and inactivity. Luckily for us, these teachers are few in number and readily identifiable. Like the bob-white or the cuckoo, they are immediately distinguishable by their call, for theirs is always the song of cheap cynicism. Fortunately, we know that cynicism is merely failure's imitation of pride, and the wise teacher ignores this advice as much as possible. These teachers most certainly should not be a part of the process of generating of expectations or standards.

All these pitfalls are to be recognized and avoided if the teacher is to oppose the natural atrophy and erosion of standards and expectations.

COMMUNICATING EXPECTATIONS

Expectations of student achievement and standards for success are relatively meaningless if not shared openly with the students. Courses should begin with a general overview of the expectations for students (in terms of behavior, personal productivity, and progress) and the standards for evaluation. Throughout the year, every specific task or project should be initiated with an explanation or model of what success looks like and how evaluation will occur.

We find the following paradox delightful. Few workers in the world have so zealously negotiated the terms by which they will be evaluated as have educators. The annual teaching evaluation is a finely crafted tool specifying every aspect of the evaluation and every ramification of every possible outcome from that evaluation. Teachers know exactly when they will be evaluated, how they will be evaluated, what will be stressed in the evaluation, and by whom. They have left nothing to chance. On the other hand (what we find to be the comedic side of the paradox) is the fact that in far too many classrooms, grades and standards are a total mystery. What we have mandated through law as our "rights" we have failed to grant to the students with whom we work even as a mere courtesy.

How does a teacher know if he or she has communicated expectations clearly? It is not difficult at all—one need only to listen. What follows are some sample comments you might hear if your expectations and standards have not been clearly communicated:

- "Well, he still hasn't figured out what you want on essays." (from a parent)
- "I studied the wrong stuff for the test." (from a student)
- "I tried to help them, but I didn't know what you wanted." (from another teacher)
- "What are we doing?" (from everybody)

It is only when students understand expectations for them and the standards by which teachers will evaluate them that we may hold them responsible for their own success and progress. The legend does not work in clandestine darkness. The legend operates in the open light. Students should not be expected to intuit goals, standards, or expectations. It should not take students a few months or a few tests to determine what a teacher is "looking for." What is being sought must be the first concern communicated to the class.

There are a few major tenets that all teachers, and certainly the legend, should follow to make sure expectations and standards are being clearly communicated.

Tenet 1

Expectations should be written out and visible to the students from the beginning of the course, the unit, the week, and every day. They are repeatedly shared as the purpose of all activities!

> *Our goal in this AP English class is to see that each of you can score at least a 3 on the exam in May; we'll do that by practicing the objective parts of the test and rewriting all essays that would not receive at least a 6 according to the assignment's rubric.*

> *By the time we finish this unit, you should be able to identify the noble gasses by their features and atomic weights.*

> *At the end of the class today, I expect you to be able to identify the four most important conditions that made war between the states inevitable.*

Tenet 2

Standards are never hidden—they are published periodically in the classroom and may even accompany important assignments. They may well have been learned by the students prior to any assessment.

> *The building's grade scale will remain posted in front for the year. It is nonnegotiable.*

Papers must be written in ink, one side of the page, and with a proper heading, as modeled in this poster, or they will not be accepted.

If you fail to show your work for every step of the solution, you will not receive full credit.

Tenet 3

Expectations are communicated in a positive fashion. Negativity is antithetical to any attempts to have students fulfill expectations. Our favorite list of "expectation busters" is below: This list provides sure-fire ways to make certain students don't succeed.

You're going to have trouble with this one.

It's only a trick question if you didn't read the footnote.

This is the easiest test we've ever had; if you don't do well on this, there's no hope for you.

What's wrong with you people?

Tenet 4

The legend chart or graphs students' progress, making their growth concrete. Too often, their own progress remains intangible to students and, therefore, they tend to become disheartened, excluded from their own success.

If you look at the front of your writing folders, you'll see that you're not writing any more sentence fragments.

On the board is a chart showing how your grades have improved so dramatically on the lab books.

On your personal growth charts, you can see how your times for the 440 have improved since we began the strength training.

Tenet 5

The legend makes certain that in class, all students participate at the same level of difficulty all the time, without excuses. There has been some tremendously insightful work done in the area of communicating expectations to students in the course of daily interchanges. A considerable wealth of research is available specifically about teachers communicating expectations. The T.E.S.A. staff development program is almost totally devoted to making all teachers effective communicators of high expectations. In a quick overview, the basic principles of communicating high expectations impartially to all students include absolute equality in each of the following:

- Frequency (no group of students receives more opportunities to answer than any other group): The legend sees to it that all students are actively engaged in learning equally, all the time. The legend avoids teaching to the "T."
- Difficulty (no group of students receives more difficult questions or questions at a higher level than any other group): Easier questions communicate lower expectations. Students everywhere pick up on that discrimination immediately.
- Opportunity (no group of students receives longer wait time or more help in determining a correct response than any other group): Teenagers hate silence. The pause during which time they are to be thinking is anguish to them. The legend uses wait time to his or her advantage.
- Expectation (no group of students receives either verbal or nonverbal indication that the teacher has higher or lower expectations for that group than for any other group): It is, after all, a rather simple rule: Any question may be asked of any student.

Simply put, every student is always equally held up to the same high expectations and standards regardless of the teacher's biases or personal expectations of that student's success. If we begin the class expecting that black students won't work well at higher levels of learning, or assuming that children of broken homes will not handle pressures well, or suspecting that girls can't do math, or believing that football players will be rhetorically challenged, we will prove ourselves right. We will communicate those beliefs to the students, and they, unfortunately in this case, still trust us enough to believe us. We must put those biases behind us; even if we cannot, we must treat all children the same all the time.

When these tenets are followed, then the legend is as continuous in communicating his or her expectations and standards to students as he or she is in seeing to the rest of the students' education. But more important, by communicating both regularly, the legend converts students into active partners in their own learning. Only then are they able to put forth their best efforts in achieving success. Logically, this entire process extends into the home as well. The better informed parents are about the expectations and standards of their children's classroom work, the better help they will be able to offer at home. Communicating expectations is every bit as important as setting them.

MAINTAINING CONSISTENCY AND OBJECTIVITY

In the emotionally troubled lives of students, in the socially convoluted experience of the entire school environment, and in light of the rapidly changing emphasis of educational thinking, there must remain the immovable rock on which students can steady themselves. That rock must be the classroom teacher. The legend is, perhaps as much as anything else, consistent and objective.

By consistency, we do not mean inflexibility, hopelessly stuck in the same rut year in and year out. The legend is not predictable. Being mechanical or habitual would, of course, contradict most of what the sections on personality and motivation have to offer. What we do mean is that the consistent teacher exhibits the following:

■ The same high standards and expectations for all students, all the time—regardless of the students, regardless of the period of the day or time of the year, regardless of the class. Whether it is in advanced placement calculus or with a substitute in physical education, students know that this teacher is going to demand the best of them.

■ The same work ethic at all times for all students. If school is important, then every minute of every day is essential, and if the students don't sense that urgency about education from the teacher, we can hardly expect them to manifest it later. Likewise, every teacher should be cognizant of the fact that students have no respect for teachers who are easily talked into off-task activities or discussions (even though they may be highly sought at registration time!).

■ The same system of rewards, punishments, and motivation is in place for all students all the time. Students will have a great deal of trouble achieving excellence if excellence itself is a shifting, vague concept. Likewise, if a class's chemistry is determined by the particular mood of the teacher on any given day, one would rightfully assume that that classroom will not be a very productive one.

Every bit as important as consistency is the quality of objectivity, and we firmly believe maintaining true objectivity is a far greater challenge to most teachers than they are willing to admit.

We all know the dangers of having favorites in a classroom. The image of the spoiled teacher's pet haunts us to this day. Stories of the coach or teacher to whose classes athletes flock for the easy grade do serious damage to the profession. On the other hand, it is ridiculous to think that whenever one meets a group larger than two people, one or two of them will not be favored over the others. It is absurd to think that a teacher won't have drastically more in common with some students than with others. Additionally, it is sophomoric to suppose that after grading a class's papers for half a school year, that same teacher would be unaware of the superior cognitive or syntactic abilities of some of the students in comparison with others.

That a teacher likes some students better than others is a given. That some students are more intelligent, creative, dedicated, talented, artistic, and so forth is merely a fact of life. What also must be equally true is that every student is treated and evaluated the same way in every situation; otherwise, the teacher has no claim to objec-

TABLE 3.1

XR	RQP	RRP	QPRPR	QQ	RR
XRR	RRP	QRQ	XPXP	PPQX	RRRQR
RRP	QPQR	RRRRQ	XX	PQPQ	RRQR
RRP	QPPQ	RRRQ	RRP	QXQQ	RRQR

Key: Q (question); R (response); P (praise); X (reprimand)

tivity. Losing the students' perception of our objectivity is calami-
tous. Nothing could more impugn the underlying lesson of what we
have to teach them: that they are indeed masters of their own fates;
they hold their own futures in their hands. If they perceive prejudice
in the class, then they have been absolved of effort, because, in their
minds, at least, effort cannot overcome preexisting bias.

Maintaining Impartiality

For the legend, maintaining an impeccable reputation of impar-
tiality is paramount to his or her efforts. A teacher can use several
activities to see that this concept of objectivity is maintained.

■ Keep track (on a copy of a seating chart with fence-posting or
some other marking technique as shown in Table 3.1) of interactions
with students, making certain positive interactions are relatively
balanced among every student in the class. This is a simple but
significant technique to ensure equality of opportunity and balance
of reward.

■ When evaluating students, use as many methods as possible
to evaluate the work anonymously without losing sight of whose
work is finally being evaluated. Typed work handed in by code
numbers and no names is a perfect method by which to achieve this
goal. The point here is not to allow expectations of students' abilities
to affect the evaluation of their performance.

Because the teacher expects Stephanie to be bright, to show
strong intuition, she may reward Stephanie with more points
than others when in fact her answer has more in common with
theirs than it has in contrast. Stephen, meanwhile, usually

doesn't do work as strong as the others, and the one time he really has shown some insight, it is overlooked, masked by the teacher's expectations for less-than-brilliant work.

In both situations, if the teacher were occasionally able to evaluate anonymous work, such preconceptions could be recognized and eventually overcome.

■ It is also important to evaluate students in consistently random order. (e.g., don't always evaluate Bob's paper after Fatima's because whoever's paper is evaluated after Fatima's always looks poor in comparison).

■ Recognize favorites (and unfavorites) consciously, making certain those students do not receive more or less attention because of personality preferences.

REMOVING THE EXCUSES

A popular word in education at this time, one that comes to us from modern psychological parlance, is *empowering*, which is used to mean the act of justifying, permitting, and even encouraging failure in others. The legend does not empower students to fail. Instead, if the legend believes in the importance of maintaining and communicating objective and consistent expectations and standards for all students all the time, then the legend must believe in the efficacy of his or her own system and must consequently remove all excuses for failure from the shoulders of students.

Responsibility 1

The first job of freeing students from excuses for failing is to make sure that nothing they bring with them to class automatically dooms them to failure. If a student cannot pass a course because of past failures, because of environmental or social disadvantages, because of learning disabilities, or because of any other handicap, then that child must not be placed in that class under any circumstances.

As a result, any child in the legend's class is assumed to be capable of passing and is held up to doing all the work necessary to pass. No work is permitted to be left undone, and no work is acceptable if completed at what is judged to be inadmissibly poor quality, for any reason. The legend begins under the assumption that all will succeed; he or she does not operate under the theory that a certain number or a predictable percentage of the students will fail. All actions are predicated on that belief.

Responsibility 2

The second aspect of removing excuses for failing is accomplished when the teacher accepts responsibility for the success of students. The legend assures students they can pass and equally assures them that were they to fail, it would be as much the teacher's fault as theirs, and, most important, he or she will not let that happen. This is a testament to the efficacy of education; it is, in the vernacular, "putting your money where your mouth is." It has always seemed ironic to consider the number of teachers who pursue programs that plan to accept a given number of failures. It makes much more sense to devise a program within which all students who do all the work will succeed. This is, after all, the age of the money-back guarantee. The legend should be able to stand in front of the class and announce, in all sincerity, that everyone who does all the work all the time will succeed in the class.

That is to say, in effect, "If you do all the homework and pay attention in class, you will pass the unit tests; and if you pass the tests, you will pass the final exams; and, of course, if you pass all those, you'll easily pass the course." Too often, teachers fail to make that connective progression clear to students. If a student does the work of the unit but is surprised by the nature of the test and ends up with a failing grade, then a covenant of sorts has been broken. The work of the unit should be solely aimed at preparing the student to pass the unit test. Likewise, the unit tests, taken as a whole, should be aimed at preparing the students to pass the final examination. Instruction should prepare students for assessment. The legend does not lose sight of this simple truth.

TABLE 3.2 Expectation Formula

If the Teacher Gives	And the Student Gives	Then We Have the Total
100%	10%	110%
90	20	110
80	30	110
70	40	110
60	50	110

Responsibility 3

Finally, excuses are removed and expectations are communicated if the teacher overtly forms a partnership with the student in working toward his or her success. Stealing from the athletic domain once again, most teachers would like their students to give 110%. The realities of math aside for the moment, what the legend really believes is that if the student will make any effort, then success is possible, as seen in Table 3.2.

Higher expectations on behalf of the teacher will overcome lower expectations of the student if the teacher is willing to be patient and to invest more than 50%. This is a partnership that will be successful.

A practical word at this point is necessary: Failure does occur. There is, as we have suggested, a fundamental responsibility on behalf of the student to control his or her own life, regardless of the choices he or she makes. This is a right that must be respected by the teacher. Students who fail to attend or students who do not legitimately attempt the work do fail. But for the legend, two things are true: First, this happens very infrequently, and second, the teacher shares the responsibility for that failure. Significantly, none of the failures are the result of the fact that the teacher has prepared the student to fail—there are no built-in excuses, no glib rationalizations or justifications to explain failure. The legend shares in both the success and the failures of students. The legend recognizes that not every student can always be reached, but that every failure is, to a degree, reflective on him or her, on his or her ability to make a difference.

CONCLUSIONS

The legend must build a reputation on a high set of expectations and matching standards that are continually and equitably transmitted to all the students all the time. Working from a vision of a final product back through well-paced techniques and activities that will accomplish that vision, the legend designs the course and sets the expectations for student achievement. While demanding the very best from students, the teacher continually models consistent and objective behavior, treating all the students the same all the time. The legend develops the course so that all potential excuses for failure have been removed. While sharing responsibility for the students' success and failure, the legend builds not only success but, more important, success with very challenging material. Success is only success if it is real, not artificially manipulated. Because the legend's success is assiduously authentic, he or she is able to build in students a self-esteem that will carry them throughout school and life.

4

PRACTICING SKILLFUL
COMMUNICATION

The legend must be a communicator. The legend's talents as a communicator precede any other considerations of pedagogy or technique. To a degree, any dedicated teacher can master a set of skills, making him or her an effective communicator. Although being charismatic may be a tremendous advantage to the teacher, being charismatic is not synonymous with being a good teacher. What is synonymous is a sound set of interpersonal communication skills.

This chapter looks at the characteristics of the legend's communication skills. Just as any teacher can to a degree mold his or her personality to be more effective in the classroom, as suggested in Chapter 1, so too may any teacher develop a greater proficiency with communication talents. These include:

- Practicing sound presentation skills
- Maintaining high interest levels
- Interacting with groups
- Interacting with individuals
- Merging pedagogy with communication practices

PRACTICING SOUND PRESENTATION SKILLS

Every teacher should be well versed in a few sound presentation skills. Unfortunately for most teacher trainees, these skills are rather inadequately covered in some general required speech course or methods course, and too often teachers enter education without a full understanding of the speaking and learning mechanism.

Our dissatisfaction with teacher-training programs goes back to our own preparation. In one of our methods classes, the teacher, who happened to be an assistant superintendent in one of the area's school districts, was conducting the class one evening and in his preparatory set raised his eyebrows professorially and asked, "All right, in review, why is it so important to learn your students' names right away?" He arched his eyebrows even higher and scanned the room for the first hint of an answerless student. His eye lit on a young lady near the entrance. He smiled and said, "You there, in the last row—by the door." The irony was not lost on us.

Needless to say, teacher training programs have improved tremendously from those days, but nonetheless, it is beneficial to point out some of the basic premises of good communication.

Premise 1: Intelligibility

The first postulate of sound communication is simply intelligibility (i.e., the ability to be heard and understood). The good teacher lectures and answers at a slightly louder than normal level. Everyone needs to hear what goes on in class, and a louder voice is harder to ignore than a soft-spoken one. This is not to insinuate that one shouts at the class; rather, one should maintain a strong volume for most of the work.

Premise 2: Variety

The second aspect of a sound voice is variety. A good speaker is not monotone, and when we use the word *monotone*, we include any voice that routinely falls into predictable patterns of expression or lacks variety of any kind—pitch, rate, volume, or stress. Nothing, other than unintelligibility, can be a worse trait for a communicator than a monotone voice, one that fails to demonstrate any significant variety of expression. It is virtually impossible to inspire or motivate students if the instructor's voice puts them into a coma. In other words, if classroom boredom is the dragon we seek to slay, then as errant knights we need first to be blessed with a well-varied voice. A well-modulated voice is possible for any speaker as long as he or she realizes two concerns.

Concern 1

To maximize our communication skills, we must consciously use a wide range of vocal qualities. Variety—not for variety's sake, but integrally tied into meaning—makes a speaker excellent. At times we speed up; at times we slow down; some times we get louder; and occasionally we use dramatic softness. We are not afraid to use a high or low pitch, and we certainly understand how the stress of our voice can clue the student into what is important. The teacher who would become a legend has studied the professional reader or professional speaker and has striven to master dramatic interpretive skills and, in turn, brings them to his or her performance in the classroom. The lesson to be learned from the actor is the lesson of silence. A pause, a moment of silence, can be a tremendous tool to establish mood, demand thought, or require attention. The legend intentionally uses a well-varied voice, modulated in such a way to enhance the goal of the lesson without drawing attention to itself.

Concern 2

Knowing that our voices are well varied, we must also understand that vocal tricks do not work. Using a soft voice to bring an unruly class to order is much like dousing fire with gasoline. Screaming to bring a class to order puts us on the level with the students, not in a position that demands respect. Vocal tricks do not work. What works is aiming at the well-modulated, intelligible, articulate, well-varied, natural voice—the kind we would prefer to hear when we are sitting in the classroom.

Premise 3: No Distractions

The third premise of effective speaking is one that, when violated, is done most unknowingly. An effective communicator is free of distracting mannerisms, both physical and vocal. Such distractions provide the students with a much more attractive, albeit annoying, focal point rather than the lesson itself. Students will begin to keep count of the number of "um's" and "okay's" rather than focusing on the lesson itself.

Physical distractions include, but are not limited to

Nervous tics

Annoying gestures

Repetitive movements

Playing with clothes or hair

Vocal distractions include, but are not limited to

Nonsense syllables

Extraneous sounds made by the mouth

Teeth sucking

Repetition of a single word (e.g., "Okay")

To become a legend, a teacher must be aware of the mechanics of his or her own presentation. Frequent peer observation from someone trusted who will point out such flaws or, even better, frequent self-videotaping can allow the teacher to see and hear what he or she may otherwise overlook. Keeping the attention of the students is requisite to an educator's success, and the first step toward that is to avoid offering any distractions.

Premise 4: Visual Cues

Inherent in our discussion of communication skills is the belief that public speaking is just as much a visual performance as an audio one. Today's students are being raised in a far more visual world than students from any generation before. The legend enhances presentations to draw on this fact. Good presentations are filled with meaningful gestures and movement that, like the vocal variations themselves, serve to reinforce the meaning and demonstrate importance. The good presenter realizes he or she must hold the visual attention of the students as well as their aural attention. He or she makes certain that not all presentation is made from the podium in front. During the presentation, movement around the room is consciously used so as to include every student—to make everyone feel that, for a time at least, he or she has a front-row seat. Like the effective voice, good gestures and movements are entirely natural and do not call attention to themselves. Instead, they emphasize, they punctuate, or they amuse—but they all focus attention on the material.

Premise 5: Diction

A fifth consideration of good communication skills involves the diction of the teacher. This is a particularly precarious area. On the one hand, obviously, the teacher's word choice must be determined primarily by the vocabulary of his or her audience. The teacher who consistently talks "above" the students, who reverts to college jargon merely to impress or, worse, because of an insensitivity to the abilities of the students, can be assured that his or her diction is not initiating much learning. The prime directive regarding diction is that language selection is predicated on analysis of the listening vocabulary level of the students. Advice about diction boils down to three tenets.

1. The legend speaks at a level of complexity readily accessible to all students in normal interaction of teaching or directing. He or she uses vocabulary that will be understood by listeners.

> To explain to students that Captain Ahab had not yet come to "grips with the exigencies of his own existence" does little good for the students. To explain that Ahab "had not yet learned the limits of what was possible for him" does.

2. The legend is certain that his or her speech draws on familiar past experiences of the students; the legend seeks to be in their world, knowing what they have seen or heard. The legend adheres to the foremost tenet of public speaking: Audiences (especially teenagers) want to hear about themselves, not about the speaker. The legend's talk is filled with references to the audience's lives and experience. In fact, nothing is more true about the legend other than he or she is a master of the analogy. The legend is able to relate absolutely any content material to analogous situations with which the student is

familiar. By thus drawing the new material into existing frameworks of past knowledge, the legend is able to guarantee that, not only does learning occur, but the existential framework of past knowledge of the student has also been extended and may be drawn on in analogous form at a later time as well. In other words, not only does learning occur, but the likelihood of more learning at a later date has also occurred. This is not true when students are expected to learn outside the framework of their experience and materials do not become part of their existing framework of previous knowledge.

> To teach about wave motion, the physics teacher brings in a slinky; to teach about Romeo and Juliet, the teacher begins with a discussion of modern gangs—the point is, the teacher begins with the lives of the students and works outward, often analogously, from there.

3. The legend consciously attempts to increase the vocabulary of students by introducing appropriate and relevant new terms to instruction or direction, defining them, and reinforcing their use intermittently throughout the course. In doing so gracefully, the legend destroys students' notions (and fears) of "big words," teaching them there are no such things a big words—just more exact words that actually simplify communication. Students learn that a larger vocabulary is nothing more than an efficient tool for precisely expressing thoughts, and what job isn't easier when the right tools are present?

> In a discussion of Marxism, the teacher must introduce the terms *proletariat* and *bourgeoisie*. They are introduced with humor: "Here are the $50 words of the day." Then, in discussion, they are used with their definitions of "working class" or "blue-collar occupations," but more and more the terms are used independently, until by the end of the unit, they are a part of the students' vocabulary.

All three of these considerations help the legend determine the most appropriate and effective language that will be used in presentations. Once one has found the level at which effective communication may occur, however, a final consideration may affect one's diction. Every teacher has an obligation to model correct, effective communication techniques. Speaking at the students' level does not mean reinforcing substandard English.

Listening to others is every child's first language experience and, arguably, the most important in fashioning language proficiency. If this is even remotely true, then teachers who reinforce substandard language or incorrect grammar do a disservice to the entire education process. The legend realizes that whenever he or she communicates (verbally or in written form), he or she models communication skills the student will mimic. Therefore, regardless of the discipline, every teacher must be expected to communicate in standard, correct English.

Premise 6: Naturalness

The final aspect of a powerfully effective communicative voice is naturalness. The good voice is free of affectations. It does not imitate others; it does not try to impress with affected pronunciation or emphasis. In fact, if a key to becoming the legend is establishing a trusting, one-to-one relationship with the students, then one's speaking voice must be real and natural. To this end, eye contact with each individual in the classroom is essential. Every time the teacher makes eye contact, he or she draws that student into the learning situation, reinforcing the idea that the teacher and student are in the process together and that the teacher cares about the success of that student. The legend has a natural, easy, pleasant, warm presentation, making all the students feel as if they are being addressed individually in a caring, honest manner.

And So . . .

The teacher wishing to improve his or her communication skills understands that everything except timbre and pitch range is subject to conscious manipulation. With study, practice, and conscientious effort, every teacher can become at least an acceptable communicator and at most, with direction and dedication, an interesting, lively, attention-demanding speaker whose presentations are free of annoying characteristics and distractions. To be an effective communicator, to become a legend, one must first be certain that one's communication skills are vibrant enhancers of one's efforts.

MAINTAINING HIGH
INTEREST LEVELS

The legend is not blah, humdrum, pedestrian, tiresome, common-place, stodgy, pompous, monotonous, flat, dreary, or dim. (Popular wisdom has it that Eskimos have 16 words for snow, a number that, according to linguists, tells us by its sheer magnitude how important that concept is to them. Checking any thesaurus, one can find at least 50 synonyms for the word *boring,* clearly indicating, with the same wisdom, how important that concept is to us.) Permitting a state of boredom to permeate the classroom is the kiss of death to the teacher. It cannot be overcome. It is measured not in how much learning occurs but in the number of classroom management problems that arise. But no classroom need be boring. There is nothing about any curriculum that is necessarily boring: There are no boring topics; there are no boring objectives; there are no boring projects—there are, unfortunately, only boring teachers. All audiences scream out, "En-tertain us, depress us, insult us, make us laugh—do anything but bore us!" Being banal, commonplace, trite, or ordinary is perhaps a teacher's capital misdemeanor.

The legend is not boring. The successful teacher is exciting, interest-ing, concerned, positive, stimulating, challenging, original, and enter-taining. Just as in determining correct diction, mastering all these char-acteristics begins with audience analysis. The legend understands his or her students, has a feel for where they are coming from, and is accurately able to estimate how they will react to certain messages. The legend is extremely empathetic to his or her students' situations. The legend understands that the day of the high school student has the potential to be the most boring day on earth. Passive reception of what others deem important for 6 to 7 hours a day is almost mind boggling, and, for students in a block schedule, a 90-minute lecture is enough to make the valedictorian consider dropping out.

Let's say it one more time—the legend is not boring. Instead he or she is the following.

Exciting

To keep class from being boring, the legend is exciting. The legend maintains a level of emotional anxiety in the class that makes inattention almost impossible. Such teachers shift gears quickly, unpredictably. The student never knows if he or she will next be called on to analyze a problem. Most important, the legend maintains this level of anxiety without ever being menacing. Students are anxiously involved, but not threatened, for the legend has proven over and over to students that no one will be shamed or denigrated in his or her classroom. The legend has raised students' FQ (failure quotient) sufficiently that they understand that mistakes happen and are perfectly acceptable—quitting isn't. Excitement about the learning experience saturates the legend's classroom.

Interesting

The legend is very interesting. He or she is primarily interesting by being interested. The interesting teacher is excited about what he or she teaches and does. Interest is contagious. One need only stare at the ceiling of an elevator to see how contagious interest is. Soon, everyone else on that elevator will have sneaked at least a glance at the ceiling to find what it was that so fascinated the instigator. Unfortunately, boredom is also contagious. If the teacher communicates a lack of interest, either unintentionally or (unimaginably) intentionally, students certainly will follow suit. But the legend, the master teacher, is passionate about the issues with which he or she works. In every interaction concerning the curriculum, the legend promotes high interest by naturally, unaffectedly, modeling high interest himself or herself. Without effort, the legend is able to make any topic relevant to the lives of students—when the legend talks about a topic, he or she is talking about the students. The legend is excited to do so. So are they. It's a simple truth: The legend loves what he or she does.

Concerned

The legend is demonstrably concerned about what's going on in the classroom. He or she is convinced of and has communicated to students the fact that possessing the skills and knowledge under study will improve the quality of their lives by making them better people, by making learning somewhere else easier, or simply by making it possible for them to do better on the next test. For whatever reason, the legend communicates the advantages to doing well on the unit under study. He or she shares the skills or knowledge of the unit in the same fashion a friend would relate the experience of having seen a very enjoyable new movie. The legend, because he or she believes he or she can help the students, conveys love for and appreciation of the set of skills or knowledge being studied. What is never in doubt is the legend's concern that all students succeed.

Intolerant of Negativity

The first three traits of the effective teacher are possible only if the teacher vigorously attacks any hint of negativity or cynicism. It is impossible to make learning dynamic in the face of negativity or cynicism. Both are the banners of failure, and the legend is more concerned with keeping them out of the class then he or she is with enforcing the housekeeping rules others spend most of their time with—rules whose penal qualities create such a strong "we-against-them" attitude that most students become honor bound not to find the material interesting. Negativity, cynicism, and apathy are education's true foes—not gum chewing or hat wearing. The legend knows the real face of his or her enemies and dynamically attacks them. Students are not permitted to cast aspersions on what is being studied. Questions are always welcomed and honestly answered, but derision is not.

Stimulating

By being intensely interesting and by recognizing the individual strengths of students, the legend is able to motivate students to go beyond the strictures of the prescribed curriculum. The legend uses his or her most effective ammunition wisely. Recognizing the strengths of students stimulates students to achievement in that area. Certainly most teachers were at one time told they were good with kids. The seed took root, germinated, and sprung into a profession— the comment was stimulating. We imagine that most math teachers were at one time in their young or not-so-young lives told with admiration by someone respected that they were good at math. This admiration became stimulation, and certainly they became even better at math. And so on. By being excited, by being interested, and by recognizing students' individual strengths, the legend stimulates students to greater growth in that area. Through positive communication, the legend stimulates students.

Challenging

No one in the legend's class is too self-satisfied, too comfortable. Were we to follow the students as they exited the legend's classroom, we would be able to see the impressions of the legend's hands visible on the students' backs. The legend pushes his or her students toward higher achievement in all communications with them. No one achieves final success in the legend's classroom, but everyone is always succeeding. The cautions here are obvious: Push too hard and the students fall on their faces; push too lightly and they tumble backward. Our advice is this: If the safety nets to ensure student success are in place and if the students have high FQs, then go ahead and challenge them. It's much easier to get people off their faces than to get them off their butts!

Original

Despite promises to the opposite, originality is not for sale. Canned programs are no longer original. Originality must be the offspring of the individual teacher's own intelligence and creativity. New ways to view things, new ways to learn, new group activities, new projects in the classrooms, new procedures, new seating charts, new materials, new dress codes, new ways to grade, and so on and so forth. The legend is a master communicator because he or she is not predictable, and attention must be paid to the events in the classroom or the student will fall behind. The first teacher in our building that put up the poster "Ya Snooze—Ya Lose!" made points with the students and commanded their attention that much more. This was not true for the fifth teacher in the building who bought and posted the sign. Nor was it true for the first teacher the fifth year she posted it. Originality is a spring of success for the arid classroom. The legend is an original.

Entertaining

Last, and perhaps most important, the effective communicator is extremely entertaining, and because perpetuating a dramatic mood through a class for an entire year is impossible, then entertaining most often means humorous. The humor does not distract from, it augments, the class's efforts to learn. The room never becomes a three-ring circus, but it is a one-ring circus and the elephants and acrobats and ringmaster and clowns are all in the center ring. The legend is a clever, funny person. He or she need not be a stand-up comedian, but he or she shows a sense of humor daily. The legend laughs with the students and makes them laugh. He or she has gone out of the way to bring entertaining material to class. Most important, the legend laughs at himself or herself more than he or she laughs at students. It is a tenet of the legend's classroom that if students may be teased, so too may the teacher; if their flaws are open to criticism, then so too are the legend's.

But beware—although humor is encouraged in the classroom, disruption is not. Neither is biting sarcasm.

Teasing may be.

The legend intuits and then makes public the fine line dividing the two. All the considerations for the effective communicator, that he or she be exciting, interesting, concerned, dynamic, stimulating, challenging, and original, are more readily achieved when presented in an aura of friendly banter. Learning should be fun. The legend is a funny person!

INTERACTING WITH GROUPS

Because most of the work done with students is done in the whole class setting, this is our first area of specific interest. Let us begin with this admonition. Little in education has added as much to its productivity as cooperative learning. Any individual teacher wishing to become the legend must acquaint himself or herself with the principles of cooperative learning. Variety is a must to the legend, and cooperative learning is a major tool toward the kind of variety and student involvement that leads to success.

On the other hand, unstructured "group" work is worse than no group work at all. This is not a book about cooperative learning, but we include this warning. Blindly putting people into groups and asking them to accomplish some goal is often more destructive than maintaining the normal classroom routine. The legend will most certainly use aspects of cooperative learning regularly in the classroom, but he or she will do so only after becoming well versed in their real dynamics.

What this section is more concerned with is interaction between the teacher as an individual and the students as a group. It occurs in normal lecture time, during discussion periods, and in question-and-answer sessions. As broad as these different types of situations are, they share sufficient points of commonality to generate a number of guidelines that the legend observes.

Guideline 1: Planning

Perhaps the first principle for group interaction is planning. There appears to be a direct correlation between the number of people with whom the legend interacts and the amount of planning that goes into the interaction. Planning takes place both before and after interaction with students, yet its very nature is frequently misunderstood. For example, many teachers, especially beginners, think they have planned for a class when they identify the day's topics. Knowing "what" is to be covered is entirely different from having planned and practiced "how" it will be covered. The planning we are discussing takes the form of the following:

- Identification of topics to be covered
- Design of how materials will be covered (lecture, group, discussion)
- Determination of how materials will be disbursed
- Rehearsal of presentation prior to the actual teaching
- Practice with any available audiovisual materials
- Design of frequent methods of measurement of student learning
- Creation of remedial activities for those not yet catching on

- Development of enrichment activities for those prepared to move ahead

Whereas the beginner may have trouble making such rehearsals realistic enough to benefit the in-class interaction, nevertheless they should be attempted. Such rehearsals will smooth out the presentation. Once again, it would be preferable to videotape a rehearsal so that the teacher may watch himself or herself as others would see him or her.

Guideline 2: Analysis

Equally important in terms of quality control of group interaction is the postinteraction analysis. We certainly understand that not everything we try in the classroom will work as well as we had hoped. A lesson may simply fail: The students may prove uninterested, the material may not be sufficiently covered, and learning is sidetracked; or the lesson may go brilliantly, and students may become highly motivated, materials are covered quickly and painlessly, and learning occurs almost spontaneously. In either case, analysis of what occurred and why will direct the success of further interactions.

This again is part of living in the loop as described in Chapter 3. Certainly, it is permissible for a first-year teacher to fail in a particular class activity. It is far less acceptable for the teacher to continue to fail at the same kind of activity later in the year or in future years. Simply put, the legend is a copious note taker—with one purpose in mind: This year's failures will not occur next year; this year's successes will.

Guideline 3: Vision

There is another aspect to the legend as communicator in regard to the group. The legend communicates with a vision beyond just the classroom. He or she communicates with awareness of the effect of what is said on parents, administration, coworkers, noncertified staff—in short, the entire educational and civic community. The legend realizes that nothing is said in a vacuum, and although not made timid by the awareness, the legend is cognizant of the fact that what he or she says will have repercussions in settings outside the classroom. What is said in the classroom finds its way into the teacher's lounge later that same day, repeated in the home that afternoon or the principal's house that night. The simple truth is that there are endless ramifications of what we say in the classroom, and so the legend always communicates with the entire educational environment in mind.

INTERACTING WITH INDIVIDUALS

Our last area of concern is interaction with the individual. It is in the individual, one-on-one sessions that the legend can gain the most meaningful ground as a teacher. It is here that students can be convinced of the teacher's sincerity and willingness to work with the student toward success. The one-on-one conference is not the time for sarcasm or for scoring status points!

Successful conferences with students can be measured by a number of characteristics.

1. Mutual respect is established. Both the student and the teacher are aware of the honest intentions of the other. The two parties agree, in no uncertain terms, of the function, aim, and purpose of the discussion or meeting. This is equally true for discussions about problem number 21 on a worksheet and a counseling session with a troubled child. There must be direction and intent for the interaction to succeed.

2. Successful one-on-one interactions are necessarily confidential. Nothing the student has to say is revealed without the student's permission, or in emergency situations, at least without his or her knowledge. The student must be informed of this unless previous dealings in the class have already established such confidentiality as a matter of course.

3. Once the legend has established the purpose and parameters of the meeting, he or she must see to it that the tenor of the

interaction is set properly. The effective communicator in one-on-one interactions is a master at making the student feel comfortable. Whereas comedy is a masterful tool for group communications, it is better to be serious here, rather than commit a humorous faux pas. The student's self-esteem is at high risk in conferring with a teacher, whether student-initiated or not, and the legend must assure the student that he or she will not lose any of that esteem or any standing as a result of the meeting. Likewise, the student must be assured of the earnest intentions of the teacher in these one-on-one meetings. This is principally achieved when the teacher maintains a serious demeanor. When asking the student to lower his or her psychological defenses, to open up, the teacher is asking the student to take a risk. It is for this reason that humor is usually inappropriate here, especially initially.

The success of these one-on-one conversations rests largely on beginning them correctly, with the correct atmosphere. The teacher is wise to begin exactly and pointedly in setting the mood and directing the conversation:

> *"Jarod, you know we're here so we can discuss the problems you've been having in class . . ."*

> *"Now, you should know, Rachael, that anything we say today is confidential; it stays in this room . . ."*

> *"Abdul, I think we can improve how class works if we can agree on some rules . . ."*

4. Once the legend has successfully met the concerns of the first three items, he or she becomes the world's best listener. The legend is friendly and attentive. Responses are not instantaneous, but follow a period of thought. The legend maintains eye contact. The agenda, the pace, the topics of the interaction are to be set as much as productively possible by the student. More important than the advice the legend can offer, the legend offers an ear—giving the student a format by which to work out his or her own problems. The real role of the teacher in these meetings is as clarifier, organizer, focuser, paraphraser, and only lastly adviser. First and foremost, the legend is a listener.

To help focus the conversation, the legend is quick to use para-phrasing techniques and focusing:

> *"So, if I'm hearing you, your real problem is not with the project itself, but with the people you have to work with?"*

> *"If we get a chance, we'll come back to the issue of your father, but for now, can you tell me again why you don't have time to complete our work?"*

> *"Well, then let me ask, what is your perception of the issue?"*

5. Successful one-on-one interactions are focused and as eco-nomical as possible. They need not aim at being overly brief, but they are not overly long. They are not necessarily terribly sketchy, but they are not terribly repetitive. Care must be exercised in seeing that the interaction moves along toward its intended conclusion. Other issues are not to be introduced; both persons are dedicated to reaching resolution. The legend must be prepared to refocus and to direct the conversation back toward completion when discussion has stalled.

6. Lastly, the interaction must end with a mutually agreed-on solution—perhaps a time and agenda for the next meeting or a contracted form of behavior or even a desired change in attitude. In fact, the two parties can even agree that no consensus was reached. Even this agreement adds closure to the discussion and validates both parties' participation in it. Just as the meeting began with an intent, the participants in the meeting must end it with an evaluation of how well that intent was achieved and what the solution reached implies for both parties.

Individual meetings provide the teacher with the greatest oppor-tunity to establish the kind of personal relationships that make any teacher a legend. It is in such meetings that trust is established, caring is evinced, and anxiety is dispelled. The unapproachable teacher has already compromised his or her own potential for success. Students turn to the legend not because they find the legend to be the most nurturing or most forgiving, but because they recognize in the legend the ability to be sensitive to their needs without risk. Teachers who are able to show such respect for their students are the ones who more quickly may command it back from them.

A last area of discussion that is very important in the area of one-on-one interaction is nonverbal communication. The wrong expression, the wrong posture, can belie anything words may say. In fact, the expert speech teacher can verify that what we say is always secondary to how we say it. There are no words whose meanings are not determined more by the tone and stance with which they are spoken rather than the lexical meanings of the words themselves. "I like that sweater" can be complimentary or bitingly critical.

Likewise, posture and expression can undo anything words may attempt. The legend is aware of this and has studied the precepts of nonverbal communication. The legend is careful not to violate any tenets and undo the message he or she has worked so diligently to communicate.

MERGING PEDAGOGY WITH COMMUNICATION PRACTICES

It becomes impossible to separate communication theory from educational practice. The method by which the teacher communicates is the method by which he or she instructs. Communication works in a broader sense to make the legend successful if he or she is aware of three remaining areas of concern.

Genuine Communication

One of the first concerns of which any teacher should be cognizant is the reality of having established two-way communication with students. Too often, teachers operate under the misconception that they are communicating with students, when in fact they are not. As the legend teaches, he or she maintains constant, real communication with the students. He or she does not ask, "Understand?" or Okay?" and let silence be an affirmative answer. That is false communication. Instead, having finished presenting tomorrow's homework, the legend turns to students and asks, "Who can tell me what the assignment is?" Receiving an answer, the legend turns to another student and asks, "What did he just tell me, and is he correct?"

The legend does not allow a single response from one of the better students to be the yardstick by which he or she measures if a concept has been mastered. Instead, the legend communicates with a representative sampling of all students and demands accurate paraphrasing and summarizing of what was to be learned prior to proceeding. The legend maintains genuine communication with the students.

Accessibility

Communication between students and teacher, as well as between parents and teacher, is possible only if the teacher has made himself or herself accessible to both groups. Problems may be averted and feelings may be salvaged only if these lines of communication are preexisting and well tested prior to a problem arising.

To make himself or herself accessible to the students, early in the year the legend will make available for student use at least the following:

- Office hours
- Home phone
- E-mail address
- Before- and after-school hours of availability
- Planning periods
- Absolute willingness for students to use all methods as they need

By implementing these lines of real communication, the teacher is taking away excuses for failure before they can be used. He or she is establishing a working relationship that will result in greater success for the student. Such a practice is more than simply good will, it is good teaching.

In addition, the teacher must make himself or herself accessible to parents. He or she does this much in the fashion by which he or she established good lines of communication with students. The legend does this by implementing and pursuing the following:

- A place and time at which parents may reach the teacher regularly
- A voice mail message with the evening's homework or unit due dates
- Regular letters home at the beginning and throughout the course
- A reputation for dependably contacting parents when problems first arise
- A clear communication of the desire to include parents in the educational process in the classroom

By achieving these goals, the teacher will more often find parents to be true allies in the process of helping students succeed. Failure to make these lines of communication available may result in the loss of such allies, or worse, the creation of additional adversaries.

Multidimensional Communication

The last tenet of any communication venue is a simple one. Oral communication is never enough. The principle here is simple. If the message is important (including rules, policies, changes in procedures, and lessons), then it is to find expression in as many modes of communication as possible—it is multidimensional to ensure the intent and the understanding of the message.

It is insufficient for the students to simply hear it, if they can see it also. Likewise, it is preferred that they write it themselves. Finally, if the message can be made kinesthetic, it is preferred that the students be forced to move it. Then the communication is far more likely to be successful. The legend is rarely satisfied with communication in only one mode of expression.

CONCLUSIONS

The legend realizes that teaching is an interpersonal profession, and, as such, demands conscious use of strong communication skills. It is an awareness that to a degree the teacher is a performer and must be sensitive to the audience's feelings. The legend recognizes that communication skills, although a boon to any professional, are a necessity to teaching. The legend understands that much of the community's and school's judgment of his or her ability as a teacher will be a reflection of his or her communication talents. As a result, the legend spends a great deal of time honing these talents.

Similarly, the legend recognizes that such communication skills carry an ethical responsibility for him or her to be an effective communicator but not a manipulator. Elmer Gantry and Joe McCarthy had sound communication skills, but without the ethical sense that is demanded of our teachers. We must direct without propagandizing; we must inspire without proselytizing. The balance is a fine one, but one that must be maintained.

5

FROM CHAOS
TO ORGANIZATION

---

*After circling the classroom several times and having patiently
looked over everyone's shoulder, making sure that each student
has understood his or her homework assignment for tomorrow,
the teacher begins to make her way toward her desk. Her desk is
the sanctuary sought during each class period. To be able to sit
down and catch that breather before the next class arrives is any
teacher's just reward after expending what seems to be the last
ounce of energy with the present class.*

*As she sits in her chair, she takes a deep breath, closing her
eyes for a brief moment. A great sense of satisfaction and accomplishment for what was achieved in that particular lesson set-
tles gently, warmly, around her. A peek reveals that every member of the class is still diligently attacking the homework. Eyes
close again and she continues to think quietly to herself "This
is the reason I became a teacher. . . . The students are really
starting to understand the material. . . . They're even asking
questions now. . . . What a great day this has been!" A smile
crosses her face. Life is good and she is ready to put things together for the next class. She opens her eyes and, even though
the students are behaving, even though the lesson went well, the
other reality of education shakes her by the shoulders as she looks
at her desk: PAPERWORK!*

> *Scattered on the top of her desk are various piles of depression—homework papers and tests that need to be graded, pink telephone notes from the office about parents she is to contact, a form to fill out from the guidance department, and mountains of pointless busy work from the central office. A memo about a special schedule for an assembly at the end of the week is stuck in a textbook; curriculum revision due dates circled on her desk pad have long since passed. There are progress reports to fill out, and to top it all off, tonight is her night to supervise the construction of the homecoming float—all perfectly possible if she doesn't take time to sleep this week.*

Little did our teacher know when she went into education that the actual teaching of classes would be the easy part of her day. Her nightmare would be the endless flow of paper across her desk, the perpetual dates when work was due, the continual barrage of meetings and other people's demands on her time. Add to this the need to prepare nightly for two or three different classes the next day, and the disorganized teacher is soon overwhelmed by it all, unable to function in the school environment.

The legend understands that an integral part of the teaching profession is one's ability to be organized. One can be atop a mountain when it comes to making classroom presentations, but at the same time be drowning in an ocean of paperwork. Keeping the balance between academic organization and clerical organization is what allows the legend to control his or her time, the most precious commodity in education.

We also know what the real problem concerning organizational skills is. Most people, regardless of how chaotic their private or professional lives may be, have convinced themselves that (a) they are not disorganized, or (b) they actually function better in a state of indiscriminate disorder.

For these people, we have developed the following self-test. We ask that you be honest with yourself as you work your way through the inventory, knowing that if you answer "Yes" to two or more of the questions then, in fact, you have a serious problem with organization (in which case you may want to call our hotline for help at 1-800-CHAOTIC).

Personal Survey of Organizational Skills

You may need to organize and better plan your professional life if you have ever . . .

10. Confused passing periods with planning periods
9. Forced your students to collate the pages of a still-warm test before taking it
8. Given a quiz over the book so you had time to finish reading
7. Put more arrows and ditto marks in your lesson plans than words
6. Instructed students to disregard the date on the test (198X)
5. Tried to convince students you colored the transparencies yellow for mood
4. Described showing a video to your first period class as "previewing"
3. Purchased a nonalphabetized dictionary just to save money
2. Given more than 75% of the class time to start tomorrow's homework
1. After a vandal breaks into your room at night, tipping over a bookcase full of books, papers, and folders, you called the principal to your room and her first comment when you pointed to the disaster in the corner was, "Oh, did you move your desk?"

Clearly, organization does matter and is a prominent weapon in the legend's arsenal. To understand better how successful teachers maintain a system under which they are able to function easily and effectively, it would help to break down the question of material management into three sections:

■ Mastering the clutter

■ Planning for the academic day

■ Organizing the postinstructional debriefing

MASTERING THE CLUTTER

There are three key areas in every classroom that a legend makes certain are organized: the teacher's desk, the teacher's workstation, and the students' workstations. Organization, in our minds, may be defined as having a system in place that allows for efficient performance of required tasks. It affects all aspects of the working day for the teacher. The term does not mean that all teachers are "neat freaks," with everything labeled, color-coded, and always in its place; however, if clutter and chaos hinder efficiency and productivity, then neatness should become a priority. Being organized does not make a teacher successful, but being disorganized can definitely make one a failure, both as a teacher and as an employee.

The Teacher's Desk

We all know that some students will be forever doomed to mediocrity and even failure because of their inability to organize their materials and responsibilities. These students especially are in need of models for effective work habits. At home they see their parents relaxing—not organizing work. So it falls on the teacher to be the model of effective work organization. The teacher's desk is the first place the teacher can model effective organization and neatness, two qualities often demanded of students. The desk is the most visible reflection of organization in the classroom, and it is our first chore to practice what we preach. Jokes like "I know where everything is!" and "A messy desk is a sign of an organized mind!" are just that—jokes, a humorous way to mask a serious lack of organizational skills. The students who suffer from disorganization already believe they can wing it through school. They need strong role models of organization, and the legend is determined to be one.

Top of the Desk

The top of the desk should always be characterized by orderliness and arrangement, all items in place around an open area left to work. It should not be a storage place for everything that is distributed during the day. On the top of the desk, the effective teacher keeps only those items that are used daily. A good rule of thumb is, when in doubt, do without. Do not keep items on the desk that are better stored elsewhere.

A set of stackable trays on the desk is a good idea as long as each tray has a single purpose. The top tray may be exclusively set aside for papers turned in by students. The wise teacher does not allow work to be handed in anywhere else—just in the one designated tray. Early in the year, the lesson must be taught—"If you're turning that in to me, then it must be set on this tray and this tray alone!" Other trays stacked on the teacher's desk should have other specific functions. The stackable trays serve little purpose if they are interchangeable in what they hold. The teacher guilty of this has done nothing more than allowed the mess on his or her desk to be in three dimensions! The other trays may be used for storing memos, attendance materials, projects due that week, and so forth. The key to the trays is that each has a single function, and that designated function is respected at all times.

Dump Drawer

To help keep the desk clear of memos, papers, and mail, most effective teachers use a *dump drawer* or tray that is nothing more than a short-term storage organizer. The dump drawer or tray is exactly what its name suggests, a dumping ground for miscellaneous materials that arrive throughout the day at times when they cannot be dealt with immediately. Rather than clutter the top of the desk with these papers, or worse, let them become lost in other piles, the information is dumped in this holding drawer or tray. Of course, the concept of a dump drawer works only if it is conjoined with another practice—the daily routine of going through all materials temporarily placed there.

Whether it is at lunch, before or after school, or during a planning period, every piece of mail, every memo, every request, every form, every piece of paper that finds its way onto the dump drawer or file is dealt with. In the ideal world, all teachers would follow the maxim "Handle every piece of paper once," but of course, none of us teaches at Ideal High School in Utopia, USA. Instead, we live with the realities of our situations and are forced to compromise the ideal with the real, so we use devices such as the dump drawer. That is not a problem as long as we religiously follow the daily routine of dealing with items placed there.

The routine is simple. As the teacher goes through the information in the dump drawer, he or she has only three mutually exclusive but all-encompassing choices of what to do with it:

1. Decide the information is not needed or wanted—at which point, the item is to be thrown away immediately. (Important note: We have nothing but pity for those people unable to throw anything away; those teachers who adopt everything ever placed in their mailboxes as their own long-lost children. It was not by chance that after God created administrators he placed a garbage can in every teacher's room—and yes, each garbage can is positioned in close proximity to the dump drawer!)

2. Decide the information is something the teacher can process easily and quickly—at which point, the item is immediately and thoroughly processed. Procrastination is wasted time, and the efficient teacher knows that time is too valuable a commodity to be wasted.

3. Determine that the information is important and is better dealt with later—at which point, the teacher will file it in a *tickler* file (Relax, it's not as exciting as it sounds) or write the information on his or her calendar blotter so that he or she can refer to it at a specific, later date.

If the routine is followed every day, then the teacher will become a much more efficient paper handler and a more effective teacher as he or she frees himself or herself from at least some of the drudgery of paperwork.

Tickler File

The third option requires yet another step of organization for the teacher. Right below the dump drawer in the desk should be a tickler file. The tickler file is a teacher's long-term storage organizer. There are various ways of organizing a tickler file, depending on how exact one wishes to be with information that is being stored for later use.

The simplest tickler file to organize is to take 12 hanging folders and label each folder with a month of the year. As the teacher receives information that won't really be needed or won't be acted on until later, the teacher places that information in the hanging file for that month. For example, say that in October a teacher receives a reminder that school improvement plans are due in February. That information is put in the February folder. Then, at the beginning of February or end of January, the teacher goes to the folder and is immediately reminded of what is due in February and when. As is the case with the dump drawer, a tickler file is effective only if the teacher checks each month's folder as the month approaches. Failure to make these monthly inspections turns the tickler file into nothing more than a well-organized tomb.

For the really compulsive types, it is possible to carry this organization obsession a step further. An extension of the tickler file is to keep 31 folders in front of the tickler file for the present month. At the end of January, the teacher takes the information from the February file and places it in the exact due date the 1st through the 28th. As other items are received that are due that month, they are placed in the due date folder or the folder for the date at which they must be begun.

The point of the tickler file is simple. Paperwork should not be the teacher's first priority, and because his or her attention is focused elsewhere—teaching the children—then a system must be in place to help the teacher deal with those still important but lower-priority matters. No one can remember when everything is due or needed. These files are a method of organization by which one may master the clutter. Being organized, the legend is apt to spend more time in pursuit of quality education rather than scrambling to turn in forms.

Rest of the Desk

In a similar fashion, other drawers in the desk or nearby files should be used for personal items, miscellaneous school supplies, and frequently used forms. Items should be clearly labeled, and the original plan of organization should be maintained. Without the luxury of personal secretaries, teachers must take the steps necessary to fulfill those duties as painlessly and as efficiently as possible.

The Teacher's Workstation

The second area that demands organized planning is the teacher's workstation. Whenever possible or practical, instructors should have a workstation close or attached to their desk. The workstation should be a place for items that don't belong on the teacher's desk as described in the previous section, but nonetheless remain essential to the working environment of the instructor. The workstation is the place for stacks of papers, computers, projects, or research books.

Maintaining a workstation is no more complicated than placing an additional table next to the teacher's desk. Using the desk, files, and a work table, the teacher is more able to create a work space, essential if the teacher does not have an office space of his or her own. Too often, however, teachers use their desk for everything, never really defining a work area and never defining an organizational scheme by which they may be secretary, accountant, correspondent, grader, and planner.

One final note about these two areas. The teacher's desk and the workstation are effective because they are used only when students are not in the class. Neither is a teaching area. The legend does not teach sitting at his or her desk. Effective teachers have separate teaching areas: a podium or lectern in front—perhaps another table— but the desk and the workstation are not teaching stations.

The Students' Work Area

The last area that bears scrutiny in terms of organization is the students' work area. When we described the teacher's desk earlier, we suggested that there may be a single tray of the stackable trays on the desk into which all student work is placed. Without exception, work being handed to the teacher never goes anywhere else. The single tray is, however, a minimal concept. If at all possible, the legend prefers to maintain a separate student workstation. The student workstation might be a place where the following activities occur.

1. This could be the hand-in point for all work coming to the teacher for evaluation. Again, this is the only place students may turn work in to the teacher. It is never placed on the desk, never given to the teacher at the teaching station, and never accepted in the hallways. Those works are too often lost or forgotten in transit. All work is placed here.

2. This might be a place where students returning from absences pick up any graded work that had been returned or handouts distributed during their absence. Work to be made up (with dates written on it) may also be picked up here. There could even be a monthly tickler file for students to check when concerned about missing assignments.

3. Most effective teachers have some method of dealing with absences in terms of content missed (not just handouts, graded work, or make-up work). Some teachers have students keep a class log recording all notes and discussion. Other teachers keep an index file of materials. Regardless, the student workstation is the perfect place for these materials.

4. If students have access to their own writing folders, lab reports, math portfolios, and so forth, then the student workstation is the ideal location for those as well.

5. The student workstation is the optimal place for the posting of grades. Students typically check their grades as often as they are updated, and the legend posts grades at least weekly in an attempt to keep students not only current with their grades but also responsible for them. The wise teacher will take full advantage of this by also posting important reminders and notifications for the students here.

6. Lastly, the student workstation is the perfect spot to locate individualized activities. Remediation worksheets, projects, and readings could all be placed here with directions for individual students, thus avoiding the embarrassing distribution of remediation materials in front of the entire class. Likewise, the student workstation is ideal for enrichment activities such as extra-credit projects, academic challenges, and articles and books to read. The possibilities are limited only by the teacher's creativity and the needs of the class. The point is, the legend uses the student workstation to expose the students to as much additional material as possible, in an intimate manner.

All in all, the organized classroom might look something like Figure 5.1.

Requisite to becoming a legend is the notion that the teacher is organized. Any organizational pattern for the room, like the one in

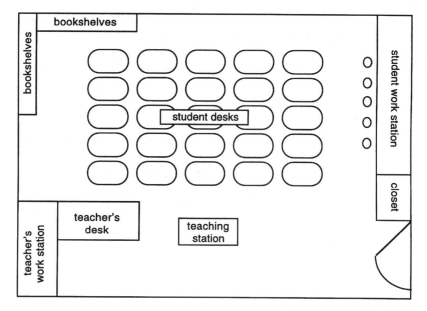

Figure 5.1.

Figure 5.1, will work; however, arranging the room is not the difficult aspect of being organized. What is difficult is maintaining the discipline to adhere to the organization, both for the teacher and for the students. This is accomplished with two resolutions.

Resolution 1

The first part is easy—the teacher must decide to follow the organizational practices he or she has designed. The semester break would be a good, first opportunity to evaluate any organization procedures and make changes then, if the old practices have proven ineffective, but otherwise the teacher models efficiency for students by sticking to the plan.

Resolution 2

The second part is not quite as easy—the students must be trained to follow, without exception, the new organizational policies. It may help to place a large poster with the rules of the workstation directly above it. Large, boldly lettered signs should indicate where papers are to be turned in and where materials are to be picked up. Likewise, the procedure for make-up work should also be posted. The students will encounter the class's make-up philosophy daily, as well as the policy for handouts and absences in general. If any kind of portfolio work is kept at the student workstation, then directions for its use must also be posted.

The intent of a student workstation is twofold. Its primary function is to help the teacher be more effective through a clear organizational plan. Second, and perhaps just as important, is to shift the responsibility to the students for make-up work, absence procedures, and portfolio management. A well-organized student workstation can end the excuses of, "Well, I didn't know I had to do it!" or "I didn't know when it was due." And maybe, just maybe, if we become organized enough ourselves, we might never again hear that phrase that sets every teacher's teeth, real or false, on edge: "Did we do anything yesterday?"

The effective teacher, the legend, designs and adheres to an organizational policy. At first it will be a chore for the teacher as well as for the students, but in a few short weeks, all will adjust to the routine and be pleased at how easily the system operates.

PLANNING FOR
THE ACADEMIC DAY

Significantly late in this chapter, we turn our attention to academic organization. Everything that has proceeded is necessary to allow the teacher to become a legend, but it will not, on its own, make a teacher one. Of course, without some kind of clerical organization, it is doubtful that any teacher would survive, much less become a legend.

Now we turn our attention to one of the most significant correlatives of master teaching: academic planning. The major components of academic organization are found in two four-letter words: *time* and *plan*. The formula is simple: the more time a teacher takes to plan, the better he or she is going to be.

We begin our discussion of time management with a stern warning: If the concepts of being goal oriented, focused, and on task aren't a part of a teacher's perceptions of effectiveness in education, then this section may be a tad threatening. Central to our discussion is the belief that the teacher, to become a legend, must be an extremely efficient manager of time. The realities of our profession necessitate it.

There is no easy way to save time during the school day, unless one can program himself or herself to stay on task with few diversions until any given project is completed. The will and drive to accomplish and finish an assignment must be generated internally: The legend is his or her own task master. As we described in Chapter 1, the legend chooses to be the best, and that choice translates into being the most dedicated. To do so, the legend maximizes the free time he or she does have.

Most free time in a school can occur during the following time slots:

1. The time before first period begins
2. The time during the instructional planning period
3. The time during lunch
4. Any time the teacher may be fortunate enough to have been given in addition to normal planning time such as a study hall, lab prep, department head time, public relations time
5. The time after school

Time Inventory

To begin an assessment of how well one uses his or her time, it is helpful to begin with a quick inventory of free time during the school day. The inventory is done by numbering 1 through 5 on five consecutive sheets of paper in a notebook the teacher carries all week long (the numbers corresponding with the categories of free time presented above).

Note: If category 4 does not apply, it may simply be deleted; if there are other categories of free time one may experience in a particular situation, then those can be added on a separate page.

For one week, the teacher is to keep a diary of the activities performed during those free times alone. At the end of the week, each page must be analyzed to see how the free time was used in that week, and what can be done to maximize the time that is available. If, on analysis, one notices a preponderance of activities such as "coffee in the teacher's lounge," "wander the halls," "watch practices in field house," or "read newspapers or magazines in library," then the quick inventory suggests an easy fix, provided that the teacher is willing to add the concepts of being goal oriented, focused, and on task to his or her permanent vocabulary.

Special note: This is not to suggest that all work and no play wouldn't drive the legend up a tree, but what is evident is that valuable time may be squandered on nonproductive activities.

If the quick inventory reveals responses such as "waiting in line for the copier," "waiting to cut letters in the library," or "waiting to get on a computer," then it would appear that this teacher is on the right track but is still wasting time. It might be to his or her advantage to be better prepared so that these things could be done all at once one night a week, when the demand on the limited facilities of the school is far less. Most waiting comes from teachers having put off preparations until the last minute, at which time they have no choice but to stand in line with all the other procrastinators. The legend not only desires to make good use of his or her time but has prepared to do so.

Closely related note: Planning well ahead relieves a great deal of the stress that compromises efforts and wastes time. The more the individual teacher can do to eliminate stress from the daily schedule, the more likely he or she will be an effective teacher.

Finally, if the quick inventory reveals responses that indicate carefully budgeted time wherein almost every minute of the day is filled productively but still there is not enough time to accomplish everything, then there obviously is a problem. In addition to adding the concepts of goal oriented, focused, and on task to the perception of education, the teacher should try to generate the courage to say "No!" occasionally as well. Despite everything that we've written so far, we have not confused the legend with the Messiah.

Final note: Even if the teacher is prepared and planned, even if the teacher is conscientious in his or her efforts, he or she must still make time for his or her own needs. The legend, out of respect for himself or herself and students, must be able to say "No!" to some requests and must be able to relax during the day. Have we just contradicted ourselves? No! (See, we can say it.)

Time Compromise

Central to time management lies the concept of compromise. It is the hardest lesson we learn as we age, but there is not enough time to do our best on everything we must do. To accomplish all he or she must in a day, the teacher cannot spend as much time as he or she would like on every lesson plan, on every project. The thoughtful English teacher would like to read every essay twice, writing voluminous comments throughout. The idealistic science teacher would like to spend 3 or 4 hours preparing every lab. The devoted physical education teacher would like additional time to get all the gear prepared and every field ready. Of course, they cannot. Merely to survive, the English teacher must finish scoring the essays in 2 hours. Just to survive, the science teacher has to limit preparations for each lab to half an hour, and that PE teacher, just to preserve 8 hours a day for sleep, will, in the time allotted only, have to do the best she can.

To do the best they can—to exist—teachers must learn to compromise their ideals with the realities of their professional existence. Each teacher may do only the best he or she can on any project in the apportioned time he or she has. The time must be wisely allotted and then wisely used. That is the heart and soul of time management and why effective planning is so critical, but still the teacher may be frequently left with the feeling he or she hasn't done the best. Regardless, that is the compromise that must be made to function as an educator. In the business world, everyone would love to have 100% success in sales, but most are happy when they are able to succeed 80% of the time, so an 83% success rate is to be celebrated, not regretted. It becomes cost-ineffective and counterproductive to fixate on achieving 100% success. This attitude is carried over to education. Striving for excellence is motivating, but striving for perfection is demoralizing.

Time for the legend is a quality that can be either an enemy or a colleague. When used well, it enables a teacher to accomplish everything he or she must to ensure success as an educator. When time is mismanaged, it is a foe, opposing a teacher's efforts and disparaging aspirations.

Anyone who experiences a great deal of success with students in the classroom knows that he or she has to be a step ahead of them at all times. Student boredom—tuning out during class—occurs the instant the instructor starts to lose focus or begins to drift during a presentation. This drifting can be circumvented only through exact planning of all aspects of the classroom enterprise. Although this has always been true, its basic philosophy is even more important in the strictures of block scheduling. In block scheduling, the teacher enjoys both benefits and liabilities. The benefits include:

- Increased opportunity for in-depth work
- Increased opportunity for individualized work
- Increased opportunity for meaningful cooperative work
- Increased opportunity for guided learning and homework
- Increased opportunity for conferencing regarding progress

On the other hand, block scheduling carries with it many liabilities in terms of planning:

- A need for more and more varied activities each day
- A demand for greater flexibility with activities
- A much finer division of time management
- A far greater amount of preparation

If planning is an obligation in the traditional schedule, it is a necessity under the block schedule. It is virtually impossible for any teacher to function in a block without far greater planning and coordination of students, activities, goals, and measurement. For experienced teachers, block scheduling requires a complete rethinking of educational approach; for novice instructors, it requires absolute dedication and readiness.

Regardless of whether the teacher operates in a traditional or a block schedule, academic planning begins with the vision described in Chapter 3. Where will the students be if everything goes as planned by the end of instruction? Because this text is primarily designed as an aid to the individual teacher as he or she strives to become a legend, we will forego a discussion of curriculum development. Needless to say, if an incoming teacher is handed an established curriculum with course syllabi and pacing charts, planning is much easier and probably much more efficient. When that is not the case, then the individual teacher must follow the guidelines presented here.

1. The first step in individual curricular planning is to determine what a successful student will be able to do at the conclusion of the year's instruction. The emphasis is not on materials (unless the vision is content specific) nor on pedagogy—rather, it is on what the student will be able to do. What else matters in education?

2. The next step is to make a course syllabus that outlines the major concepts and objectives that will be covered in the class. The concepts and objectives are almost always divided into topical units, although the organization of the skills to be mastered is up to the individual teacher.

3. To ensure that all objectives are mastered, the next step is to create a pacing chart. The pacing chart allows the teacher to visualize the sequence in which things will be taught and how much time will be allotted to each concept or objective. Experience suggests that building in review days and testing days is mandatory. In fact, the wise teacher often builds in a few extra days with each unit of study. In education, one can always count on the unexpected: assemblies, achievement testing, remediation, and so forth. These "extra days" are never free days, and if they are not needed for anything may be used as enrichment days—but they too are task oriented.

4. Once the teacher has determined the course content (syllabus) and pacing chart, the next step is to begin construction of actual lesson plans, plans that keep the students interested (not bored), make students active learners (not passive learners), and keep students on task (not just busy). As a teacher begins to fashion a lesson, he or she would be wise to keep the following direction in mind: If students are engaged in meaningful learning activity, they should be able to answer any of these questions at any point in the unit:

1. What am I doing?
2. Why am I doing it?
3. When will I be done doing this?
4. How will I know if I have succeeded?

Presentation of all material should be done in light of these four concerns. If we are to ask students to take responsibility for their learning, then we must keep them fully informed of the educational process. When they are fully cognizant of these four aspects of the learning process, then they are more likely to see the big picture of learning, and their focus is most likely to be high.

5. The final step in planning is the determination of assessment and suitable remediation. There are two important considerations about assessment. First, the more often assessment occurs, the more assured the instructor can be that no one is lost, wasting time in class. Second, the more authentic assessment is, the more meaningful it is. Likewise, it is important to note that remediation activities are more productive if they are along the lines of a different learning avenue than the original instruction. The more similar remediation is to original instruction, the less likely it will result in any improvement.

With lesson plans completed, the teacher now has put the finishing touches on his or her vision. By careful organization and planning, and by never forgetting the key concepts of being goal oriented, focused, and on task, the teacher is ready to succeed in the classroom. There remains only the realization of the vision.

ORGANIZING THE
POSTINSTRUCTIONAL DEBRIEFING

As the teacher works through the first year of instruction under a new curriculum or a new scheduling format, it is critical that two final steps are taken in addition to the clerical organization and academic planning that go on. While he or she works (sometimes flies and sometimes stumbles) the way through the year, the effective teacher maintains a well-organized file system for every unit, subunit, or daily lesson taught. No originals are thrown away. All the teacher's notes, all handouts, all syllabi, everything that was used or planned, is kept in a carefully organized and labeled file system that allows immediate retrieval later. There is no need to reinvent the wheel every year.

By keeping materials and intricate debriefing notes on the success of the lessons, the legend is able, to a degree, to win back some of what was lost by the compromises he or she had to make to the realities of limited time. Now, in year 2, the teacher can check notes, make any improvements or changes deemed necessary from last year's work, and present an even stronger unit. That improved proficiency is possible only through diligent debriefing and organization.

A special note needs to be added. As beneficial as the above plan is intended to be, it contains the possibility of a great educational transgression. The teacher who teaches the same unit year after year with the same handouts and the same quizzes and the same readings and the same exams is as guilty of not planning as is the teacher who does nothing more than "wing it" day to day.

So how does the legend balance these opposing directions?

First, files are kept, but they are kept in a series of systematic debriefings. Before anything is returned to the file, it is reviewed and analyzed. What worked? What didn't? What should be done differently next year? Everything is always dated. That is a subtle discouragement from using the same material next year. Students like to point out teachers' foibles, and lethargy is one of their favorites.

Second, a careful item-by-item analysis of any measurement devices is done, with results written on the only copy of the material filed for future use, once again discouraging blind reproduction of materials in following years. The purpose is to create a one-two punch that will help the teacher move toward being a legend. The wise teacher saves everything, but only after analyzing its success in light of the concepts and objectives that originated the planning at the beginning of the year, and then saves it in a manner that forces him or her to reformat it before using it again.

Now the cycle is complete, and with the carefully analyzed materials from year 1, the teacher is ready to go back and redesign the concepts and objectives for the next year as well as restructure the syllabi and pacing charts that will make next year's experience even more successful. It is only in a regimented cycle as described here that real growth for the teacher is possible, and the cycle is plausible only if the teacher has maintained a strong system of organization.

CONCLUSIONS

Many students find organization of their own materials and lives difficult for a host of reasons. The classroom teacher who models organization by presenting curriculum in an orderly manner enhances student learning for all students, especially those who have difficulty processing information. An organized teacher sorts, labels, and connects facts so that curriculum has meaning and relevance. An organized approach to learning enhances meaning and stimulates more facile retrieval of information at a later date.

Even if a classroom teacher is not the most organized teacher in the building, he or she can still give the illusion of organization, communicating an atmosphere of stability in the students' lives. It is the atmosphere under which efforts will be maximized and results will be more readily achieved.

6

RECOGNIZING AND PROMOTING EXCELLENCE

Walking down the hallway at school several years ago, a volley-ball coach stopped the athletic director to raise a concern about her athletic program. She questioned why someone hadn't been promoting two of her successful athletes. Her statement went something like this: "I can't believe that no one has put an article in the paper about Cheryl and Kelly! Doesn't anyone care about my program?"

At a faculty meeting, a staff member explained how he used bonus points or extra credit to promote the idea of doing more than the minimum with his students. Another staff member quickly went on the attack: "That sounds like bribing the students to do their work! Isn't our job to motivate the students—make them want to learn? What's the real lesson we're teaching here?"

Several years ago, a middle school teacher made out a purchase order for various supplies for the coming school year. Included in her order were several sheets of scratch-and-sniff stickers. Weeks later, her request form was returned with almost everything approved—only the scratch-and-sniff stickers had been red lined by the business department. The business manager attached a note. It read "Those items are for elementary teachers!"

Enough examples? We think so too, but the message is clear: Educators may very well fail to understand the power and significance of recognizing and promoting excellence. It would seem that the major myth of education is that the students should bring to the class with them an inherent love for learning (and especially a love of learning in the teacher's field) and when they don't, well, that is a problem, so goes popular wisdom, that is beyond the teacher's sphere of influence, isn't it? So the teacher throws his or her hands skyward and complains, "What can anyone expect us to do with a classroom full of unmotivated pupils? How can we teach them?"

The answer is obvious. We cannot.

We cannot teach them until we have motivated them. The legend differs from many other teachers in this especially: The legend takes on himself or herself the responsibility for motivating students. If the students are unmotivated, it is because they have not yet been motivated, and that too is a major part of the legend's job. Motivation is such an important facet of becoming an educational legend that we have dedicated the entire next chapter to it.

This chapter, however, deals with a specific kind of motivation—recognition of success.

Teachers are, without a doubt, the least commercially crass people in America. The classroom is as far as one can get from Madison Avenue, but that is not to say that there are no lessons for us in the business world. In almost every industry to which one turns, one finds that outside of operating costs, the biggest investment is in marketing. It often outstrips even research and development. Why? Simple— American business is based on motivating consumers, and its success in doing so is unmatched in history. Business promotes itself.

That lesson learned, the legend understands and uses the power of recognition by promoting success, wherever it occurs, in the classroom. A closer look at recognition reveals how the legend is able to use it effectively to further motivate students and achieve even greater success. To be a successful device, recognition encompasses four standards:

- Making recognition visual
- Safeguarding the honesty of recognition
- Keeping recognition measurable
- Extending recognition beyond the classroom

MAKING RECOGNITION VISUAL

His name was John Gorrie!

The man who did more than any other human being in promoting recognition of excellence in education invented the refrigerator in 1844.

There are not many homes in which the refrigerator does not serve a far greater function than the preservation of foodstuffs. It serves as a place to display school work graced with anything from gold stars and smiley faces and hymns of personal praise to A+s. For every refrigerator so decorated, there is a proud little (or not so little) girl or boy who three, four, and five times a day sneaks a peek and a grin at the visual proof of her or his worth.

What most elementary teachers have always known and practiced is the fundamental art of successful recognition. Yet what we at the secondary level frequently fail to understand is the basic canon of such recognition—it must be visual, something more than a passing comment of "nice work" or "good job." When a student has something in hand that he or she can take home, put in the locker, show to a friend, use as a book mark, or possibly see on a wall, that student is rewarded a hundred times more than the recipient of verbal praise. What is stressed here is that the reward, the recognition, is visual, and whether the student elects to have it displayed for all to see or hidden away where only his or her eyes will see it, visual recognition has longer and therefore greater capacity for establishing self-esteem and increasing the likelihood of further success than mere aural plaudits.

The token or artifact of recognition may take any form as long as it is visual. It doesn't have to be, but may take the form of any of the following:

- A certificate
- A rubber stamp
- A golden seal or star
- A prize pencil
- A coupon for free stuff
- Any trinket or toy
- A cartoon

- A can of pop
- A simple smiley face

Regardless of its form, as long as the value of such recognition is defined beforehand, its visual representation will accomplish the goal of rewarding outstanding effort or identifying success and motivating its recipient and others toward further achievement.

Without doubt, the cynic now is asking if such recognition is only for the young. Will adolescents scoff at such recognition? The answer to such skepticism may lie in the following examples.

For over a century, the Boy Scouts of America have recognized the need for visual, physical recognition. Thus, the scouts offer merit badges as proof of accomplishments.

College football teams across the nation offer stars, logos, and sometimes even skulls for their players to paste on their helmets as proof of their success.

When we were first approached with the idea of a "wall of fame"—the posting of names of individuals who reach a certain level of success, say 90%, on major assessments—we too were a little dubious of how students would react to it. But soon the efficacy of such a program of visual recognition was made clear: Every student in every class, including the advanced placement classes, believed having his or her name placed on the wall was a matter of grave import. If one thought he or she had unjustly been left off the wall, the student complained; sometimes parents complained. Students spoke of preparing thoroughly enough to "make the wall." The wall of fame, as a visual recognition of success, had achieved its purpose—it rewarded, it motivated, and it made the abstract (student growth) a little more concrete.

Recognition of success is not juvenile—in fact, it is what we all expect from life, and the wise teacher, in a nonthreatening manner, takes full advantage of this most common human desire.

The key point to remember is that the legend takes the time to recognize students. The legend never assumes that someone else will take the time to validate a student's efforts or successes. The legend knows that we all grow best from our successes, not our failures, and that regardless of how small, every success must be celebrated. Criticism can be verbal; it can be short-lived (in fact, it's best if it is); but recognition for the job well done should be long-lasting, permanent. It's why we keep scrapbooks. We don't want to let any of our victories slip away. The successful teacher knows that and capitalizes on the universality of that feeling by providing visual recognition for all victories. Such recognition is not done whimsically. It operates carefully within the considerations set forth in the remainder of this chapter.

SAFEGUARDING THE
HONESTY OF RECOGNITION

Although other teachers may attempt to use visual recognition of student success, their efforts may never seem to come to fruition. This may especially be true when they violate some of the basic principles of using visual recognition.

Promoted

One of the factors that may separate the legend from other teachers is not necessarily the type of recognition awarded, but how the recognition is promoted by the legend. The legend knows that the key to successful recognition is in the promotion of the award. The legend promotes the award and therefore the program, and by doing so lends a great deal of prestige to the recognition itself.

- It is promoted throughout the classroom.
- It is promoted throughout the school.
- It is promoted throughout the community.
- It is promoted in the home.

When a student takes home that special recognition, he or she will find much more praise if his or her parents have already been informed of the worth and merit of such an award; otherwise, they are somewhat at a loss about how much or what kind of praise to lavish on their child. Not only has the legend designed a strong system of reward using visual recognition, but he or she has also promoted it so that when a child is recognized, others may appreciate the value of such recognition.

A perfect example of how such promotion is accomplished is the varsity athletic letter. One need not ask many athletes of any sport what the requirements are to letter in that sport before receiving an accurate answer; it is an award to which most sport participants aspire. And, because they believe they can achieve it, they know the standards they must reach to win the distinction. Likewise, the school recognizes what a letter signifies, as does the community at large. The desirability of the letter and its value are possible only when the award itself has been expansively promoted.

Regardless of whether it is a schoolwide program such as varsity athletic letters or honor roll or a classroom honor, the award itself, along with the standards it satisfies, must be promoted and publicized to achieve true merit in the eyes of the students.

Valued

Inherent in the discussion on promotion is the concept of the recognition's value. Unless the award is valued to some degree, it will achieve none of the functions for which visual recognitions were designed.

The value of visual recognition, regardless of its form, lies in adherence to several principles, the first of which is honesty. Its final worth is subject to the same kind of supply-and-demand machinations that determine price in the world of commerce. If recognition is awarded for completion of any task, regardless of how modest, then the marketplace (classroom) is soon flooded with what are now rather worthless trophies.

This is nowhere better seen than in the availability of computer-generated certificates. At one time, a certificate of achievement was a very impressive award. It had been prepared by a local printer, often was framed, and was taken home with a great deal of well-deserved pride. Whether presented in the athletic, academic, attendance, or behavior venue, certificates were highly prized by students and parents. But with the proliferation of PCs, the ease with which one could generate personalized certificates has lessened their value.

The third certificate for good spelling sent home in the first quarter of the year lessens the value of the first two, and soon the certificates, if taken home at all, are not accompanied by the pride with which they once might have been.

The awards must be honestly conferred to truly deserving students who have met estimable levels of success. If they are not awarded according to high enough standards, they lose their value again because of the frequency with which they are awarded. The lesson here is clear: If the visual recognitions are bestowed too freely, too often, they soon lose their value.

Meaningful

The legend is well aware of the concerns for value, but he or she is also aware of the opposite concern: If awards are not made frequently enough, they may lose their meaning. If, according to the standards by which these visual recognitions are awarded, they rarely appear and then only regularly to one or two of the better students, then they lose their meaning for the entire student body just as easily as if they are awarded too frequently.

If such awards are viewed by the students as impossible to achieve for most, then it will be necessary, according to the rules of teenage self-esteem, to devalue them—for that which is unobtainable must, according to adolescent ego, be demeaned.

Determining how and when to award recognition for work well done is a high wire the teacher must walk, demanding rigorous balance, an equilibrium painstakingly sustained by the legend.

Balance

To return to the analogy of commerce, the legend constantly reads and studies the marketplace of the classroom as well as the consumers that make up that marketplace so as to maximize the effectiveness of a visual recognition program. When self-esteem is low and students aren't making academic progress, the legend might offer a special promotion to invigorate the marketplace. Awards might be offered for a certain percentage of improvement on a make-up test. A key homework assignment might be highlighted by offering visual recognition for success on it.

Regardless of the strategies employed, the important aspect is that the legend maximizes the effectiveness of visual recognitions by manipulating the frequency with which they appear so as to maintain their value in the classroom. It is only then that they most effectively serve as a tool of motivation and a source of self-esteem; however, at no time does the legend lower standards just for the sake of giving recognition. Such a combination of both flexibility and constancy is why students respect and admire the legend the most! When the student needs to be fired up but still has to meet the standard of success that was set for excellence, the earned recognition will have its most cherished value!

KEEPING RECOGNITION MEASURABLE

The old saw "What gets measured gets done" is a sentiment everyone needs to cherish deeply. If a teacher wishes to make sure that a program of student recognition occurs and succeeds, he or she must have a system in place to measure its effectiveness. The procrastinators in education will always want to do it: They'll be excited about how they will institute it, they may even draw up plans for implementing it, but as the realities of other expectations and duties press on them (also having been postponed until later), such a program will never be realized.

In the meanwhile, the legend will have created a program for visual recognition, determined a timetable of implementation, and designed a system of feedback by which to evaluate its success and make subsequent modifications of the program as it is being used.

The first aspect of a recognition program design is the planning. Rather than starting in a void, it would be wise to look for a model by which to design the program, and, luckily for us, a very successful model of recognition already exists. That model is found in the video game industry. Virtually any video game (for the sake of good taste, we will ignore that genre of video amusements whose fun comes in tearing out another's heart) has a number of consistent elements:

- Colorful graphics exploding on the scene
- Well-defined levels of achievement
- Consistency of reward
- Potentially long-lived recognition

Colorful Graphics

Video games are colorful and stimulating; the teacher's visual recognitions should be also. They should feed on the interests of the day: athletic teams' successes, current hit songs, popular movies—all related to the class, of course. If certificates are awarded, they should be colorful, with graphics and style. Entertaining pencils, pins, and so forth are the rule of the day. The first improvement video games made after the innovative but monochromatic Pong was the inclusion of colorful graphics; teacher recognitions should do likewise.

Well-Defined Levels of Achievement

The levels of achievement must be well promoted, and to be well promoted, they must be well defined. In video games, levels of achievement are clearly publicized on the screen. Players compare themselves based on the levels they have achieved; with the attainment of each new level, bonuses are awarded. The exact same situation exists in the legend's classroom. Standards are set forth by which achievement will be recognized.

For example, the teacher may do any or all of the following for an upcoming test:

- Award a designer pencil for scores of 85% and better
- Place names of those scoring 95% on a wall of fame
- Allow students with perfect scores to design their own "boaster poster"
- Recognize anyone whose score is an improvement of 10% over the previous test with a certificate of improvement, suitable for framing

Special note: This final type of recognition may seem to be at odds to our earlier discussion of standards, and to a small degree it may be, but by its extremely finite nature, it is an acceptable, temporary compromise. A slow-starting student may earn one or two of these, but soon must graduate to the other levels of recognition to continue to receive any awards.

Of course, recognition need not stop there. Special recognition for those repeatedly achieving high levels may be defined as well. The point is to define clearly the diverse levels of achievement worthy of recognition. Video games offer players a chance to type in their names next to a high score. One need not be around children and games long before seeing how effective a motivational tool that is. One need not have much imagination to imagine how much more effective such devices in the classroom can be.

It is in this area that the question of standards must again be addressed. As suggested earlier, recognition loses its value if it is too easily or too rarely won. The teacher is expected to set legitimate standards by which to award such recognition, but at the same time, he or she is expected to be prepared to evaluate the success of the program and perhaps be willing to redefine the levels of achievement necessary for success to be recognized.

Consistency of Reward

Video games deliver on two promises: instant and consistent recognition for success. It matters neither who plays nor when. Success is always instantly recognized. These two concerns are also integral to the program of recognition in the classroom. Once the program has been designed and the standards of excellence have been defined, the next part of the design is probably the most difficult—the delivery. Consistency is the key element at this level. Nothing will destroy a recognition plan more quickly than for the students to perceive the teacher to have backed out on a promise or to have failed to come through with the anticipated reward. After the levels of achievement have been defined and promoted, it is incumbent on the teacher to see that recognition always follows success.

Likewise, lack of instantaneous reward is another flaw that can cause the demise of the program. As in the case of returning graded tests or homework, once a day or two has passed and the recognition has not occurred, the student's perception must surely be that it just wasn't an important activity, success was not really meritorious, or worse, the teacher doesn't really care. For a program of recognition to be effective as a builder of self-esteem and, therefore, a motivator for future success, the issue of consistency is not negotiable. Every success is met with consistent and instantaneous recognition. Always.

Potentially Long-Lived Recognition

The final component of the video game industry to be transferred to the classroom is to make the visual recognition potentially long-lived. Generating a sense that this achievement could be appreciated for years by future classes gives the recognition a worth surpassing all else that could be done within the confines of that school year alone. This can be achieved in any number of different venues:

- A permanent wall of honor

- A hanging plaque

- A showcase of pictures

- Booklets with records of achievement

This list is limited only by the imagination of the teacher. Likewise, along with being long-lived, the visual promotion should be personalized whenever possible to the subject matter or the task being recognized. The more unique, the more special and long-lasting, the more effective the recognition becomes with students, especially if there is the chance that the success can be seen by many others.

A plan of visual recognition is an essential tool that the legend uses effectively to honor students who have dedicated their time and talents to meet the standards of excellence that have been set in the classroom. Promoting academic successes and recognizing accomplishment is unfortunately an Achilles' heels in education today. We all know it should be done, but there never seems to be enough time in the day to do it. Students enjoy competition (especially competition that recognizes winners and does not discredit losers); and students enjoy being recognized for their success, especially when the recognition is well earned. All teachers need to capitalize on those shared feelings.

EXTENDING RECOGNITION
BEYOND THE CLASSROOM

The farther recognition is promoted beyond the single classroom, the more effective a device it becomes. Once the teacher has implemented classroom levels of recognition and promotion, the greater challenge remains: promoting those successes outside the classroom to the school and community. A little extra effort will pay large dividends if the teacher takes the time to delegate some of the responsibilities to the students for this part of the recognition plan. By delegating responsibility for at least part of the communitywide promotion to the students, the teacher has apportioned ownership to the class itself, and with ownership comes commitment.

Schoolwide

In the school community itself, congratulations in daily announcements can give schoolwide recognition, if, and only if, permission by the recognized student is given. The problem with this approach is its inherent weakness in not being visual and, therefore, being very short-lived. To promote the program outside the classroom, the main focus or effort should be toward creating impressive visual displays in well-traveled hallways. Such displays can be centered around a theme or a logo, displaying records, student work, and pictures. They serve notice to the entire school of the successes of the classroom and the students. They meet all the requirements for successful recognition promotion.

Communitywide

The last step is to promote a recognition program to the community as a whole. Again, the recognition or promotion must be visible. An article in a local newspaper by itself will be lost in the other school news, but an article with graphics will stand out. In addition, the legend understands that the electronic media holds strong potential for recognition campaigns. Local radio stations and often local television stations actively search for stories involving successful students; such stories help the stations fulfill their mandated Federal

Communications Commission community-service requirements. Finally, many local businesses are willing to sponsor a limited number of rewards such a coupons or free merchandise (if dispersed by the teacher in a meaningful manner) to successful students. The legend makes use of all community-oriented possibilities.

Aside from the benefits to the recognition program, such multimedia campaigns serve a more important function as well. Parents, especially at the secondary level, continually complain about being left in the dark in regard to what is happening that is "positive" in school. Too many times, rumors about bad situations are the only topics of conversations in the grocery stores or the post office or in the editorial articles in the local paper. School strikes, taxes, suspension records, taxes, expulsion cases, and taxes: These are the stuff by which schools are known to most of the community.

Education has never promoted its success stories to the community well. At times, schools seem embarrassed to tout their own triumphs. Pressure may exist not to celebrate strong teachers' successes because of undesired pressures that might be placed on peers who have not manifested such victories in their classrooms. Clearly, however, this is a skewed value system. We ought to be more concerned about building the self-esteem of the students and the positive image of the school than fearing to affront the less successful teacher.

Those concerns aside, the final part of the program is to extend the recognition of student success beyond the classroom: first to the schoolwide community, then to the public in general. It is then, and only then, that the benefits of such a program may be truly realized.

CONCLUSIONS

At the very foundation of the legend's approach to education is the belief that if we expect our children to succeed, then we ought to recognize that success. More time and effort should be placed in celebrating victory than in lamenting failure. The adage that we learn from our failures has its merit in terms of effort and concepts such as failure quotient, but otherwise, the adage may do more harm than good. The need for recognition is implicit in the following story.

Several years ago, there existed an average (if not lackluster) sophomore English student. He wasn't a troublemaker, but he wasn't much of an academic success either—he was part of the great gray majority: not strong enough for classroom kudos and not weak enough for special services. He was merely getting by, slipping through the cracks.

He was, however a basketball player, a good basketball player—a starter on the varsity basketball team. That particular season happened to be a very good one, and as the team approached the playoffs, it had put together a 20-game winning streak. The streak, unfortunately, came to an end with a heartbreaking loss to one of the state's top-rated teams. After the loss, the boy was asked to do an interview by a local radio station, and in response to interviewer's questions, he reported his feelings about the loss as well as his analysis of the game.

The next Monday, before class began, he was pulled aside by his English teacher, who went out of her way to compliment him on the articulate, intelligent fashion in which he had represented himself. He, of course, could not even have imagined her listening to the ball game, much less complimenting him, but that recognition was a pivotal moment in his development, after which his grades and his attitude about school (even English) changed dramatically. It had become, like the basketball court, a place where he could win recognition—it was another place in which he now believed he could succeed.

We learn best when we believe we can succeed. We learn to believe in ourselves, in our own abilities. We form higher expectations for ourselves. We panic less quickly, assured that we will, in the end, succeed. The legend knows more than anyone that success breeds success, and such a belief ought to be at the heart of an extensive recognition program that identifies and celebrates students' victories.

7

MOTIVATING HIGH STUDENT ACHIEVEMENT

Not so long ago, a disgruntled boot camp drill instructor approached a private who was supposed to be performing a disciplinary activity. As the drill instructor neared the private, who had done absolutely nothing, the private snapped to attention.

"Son," began the drill instructor, "what were you supposed to be doing with that shovel you were just leaning on?"

"I was supposed to be moving the dirt from this trench to a pile on the far side, Sergeant."

"That's right, but as I look here, do I see any dirt moved?"

"No, Sergeant, you don't!"

"And why have you failed thus far to move the dirt from this trench to that pile, Son?"

The private, a little more than a bit nervous, could only offer, "It didn't want to be moved, Sergeant."

Motivation is, without question, the most complex and challenging issue facing teachers today. That's probably why we've left it almost until last. Like the reluctant private's defense in the opening anecdote, the sentiment "I'm a good teacher, but the students just aren't motivated anymore!" (sung to the tune of *Anything You Can Do, I Can Do Better*) is the swan song of American education.

Attempting to address the problem, school districts spend large sums of money each year to bring in consultants and entertaining speakers supposedly versed in the secret art of what it takes to unlock the mysteries of student motivation. Although most are amusing during the day-long workshops, such speakers are rarely seen or heard from again once the day's work is complete.

As they promote their particular *ism* of the year, their audiences are, at best, skeptical of people who no longer teach in a classroom themselves telling others how to motivate students. Without significant reinforcement, whatever strategies they offer are (in varying degrees of rapidity) forgotten or ignored, and the problem of motivation is left unaddressed.

The real problem with motivation, of course, is that everyone is looking for a single and simple answer. Teachers search for that one pedagogy, that one theory that, when exercised, will make all students want to do their homework, come in for after-school help, and score well on their tests and report cards. Unfortunately, and realistically, motivating students yesterday, today, and tomorrow will never be a singular or simplistic process. But a teacher wishing to be a legend can manipulate the educational environment in such a way to make student motivation a part of the regular classroom routine. This can be realized through examination of the following concerns:

- Establishing the foundation
- Adding grain by grain
- Building on the foundation

ESTABLISHING THE FOUNDATION

Motivation must begin not with the student but with the teacher. Our rule of thumb for motivating students is a simple one. The very first time, and every time after, that students enter the classroom, the legend must build and continue to build a personal relationship with each student. Before motivation can take place, a strong foundation of mutual trust and respect must be laid. That foundation is possible only when based on personal relationships with every student. Whether in a traditional schedule where each day consists of as many as six or seven classes of more than 20 students each or in a block system of three classes of around 25 students, it's easy to imagine how complex and challenging it can be to build this strong foundation on an individual level. It becomes even more mind boggling when considering the unique personalities and needs of each individual. In fact, it is the needs of the individual that must be fulfilled before learning will ever matter.

> Not too many years ago, a junior high school teacher was given a slight change in his schedule: Instead of having the 8-1s for homeroom, he was now assigned the 8-23s. The homerooms were ability grouped, and everyone in the school knew that the 8-1s were the school's sharpest kids—go-getters, successes. Everyone also knew that the 8-23s were at the opposite end of the spectrum—slow, challenged, and often unhappy.
>
> But the junior high school teacher was not at all deterred. He had not given up hope on anyone, and he announced to his homeroom students that, as he had every year with the 8-1s, he would begin the year with a weekend barbecue at his house for all his homeroom students. After a brief flirtation with joy, their faces slowly eroded back to their normal wary and weary expressions. He was at a loss. Never before had his offer for a party been so coolly received.
>
> After homeroom, a single boy approached his desk. Unable to wait to hear what the boy wanted, our teacher asked, "Why was everyone so sad? Aren't you excited about the barbecue?"
>
> "Oh, yeah, we like the idea, but after we talked it over, we knew you'd rather have the 8-1s over. And, well, it's okay with us if you ask them instead."
>
> It was obvious, even to the teacher, that recognition for these children couldn't wait for their success in the classroom— it had to begin with recognition of them as people now, people who mattered. He had to address their fragile egos and their notions that they could not live up to anyone's expectations.

There is no better venue than one of repeated, sincere recognition of students' worth not only as students but as human beings as well.

To become a legend, to make a difference in a child's life, one must build a foundation on which meaningful motivation is possible. Doing so is the result of adhering to several general approaches.

Approach 1: Convey Enjoyment

Although daunting, to say the least, establishing a personal relationship with so many students is not impossible because of a simple truth: Students will always, deep down, want to be successful and want their teachers to approve of them. Building on this knowledge, the very first strategy for laying the foundation on which motivation may be built is that the teacher must, even on the very worst of days, convey to the students that he or she enjoys being with them and having them in class. A warm smile that greets students along with brief individual or group conversations with them about their activities, hobbies, music, or movies will help to bring the teacher closer to the students' personal world. It is very important that every teacher attempt to find a little time, even if it is just in greeting the student on the way into class, to try to touch the lives of every student in some way. Such conversations are not a waste of time, they are an investment in time.

> As a self-test of how well she has accomplished this approach, the caring teacher need only look down any row in the classroom. As she comes to each student, she asks herself if she can name the topic of casual conversation he or she would cover while walking down the hallway with that particular student (other than issues related to class work). Looking down the first row she knows that she could talk about this year's football squad with Adrian; he's a linebacker. With Kim, she'd talk about movies; Kim's almost as much of a movie buff as she is. With Sasha, she'd talk about dance because she knows Sasha goes to dance lessons every Tuesday and Thursday evening. But with Megan, our teacher just doesn't know.
>
> Obviously, she has entered Adrian's, Kim's, and Sasha's worlds—but she has not touched Megan's. She may be nothing more than a teacher to Megan, a dispenser of information and discipline. The likelihood of successful intervention with Megan is far less than with the other three—so too is the likelihood of meaningful motivation.

The question of establishing personal relationships with students is further complicated by the normal demographics of any class. For argument's sake, let's begin by accepting this breakdown of a very positive, somewhat atypical secondary class setting.

> Fifty percent of the students come into class ready to learn, in emotional sympathy with the teacher sharing his or her values already.
>
> Twenty-five percent of the students come into the class uninterested in what must be done that day, unmotivated to behave or learn.
>
> Twenty-five percent of the students are fence sitters. They will follow the lead of the classroom, in whichever direction it may go.

The common error is for the teacher to spend most of his or her interpersonal time building stronger relationships with the first group of students, the 50% group. Such efforts are clearly unnecessary. These students are already prepared to learn, already motivated. When effort is spent with the first group only, 50% of the students remain unmotivated to proceed. The fence sitters are still fence sitters, and the uninterested are even more uninterested because they have again been reminded they are not in the inner group of appreciated students.

The relationships that matter most are the ones formed with the second group of students. There lies the opportunity for real success. As the teacher shows each member of the second group that he or she is interested in each one despite their reluctance to be motivated, then they become less uninterested and more like the 50%'ers. Meanwhile, the fence sitters become more noticeable as being uncommitted and are far more likely now than ever to join in. All teachers benefit by forming personal relationships with their students; the legend is simply more aware of how establishing relationships with certain students can promote even greater success for the entire class.

Simply put, the legend seeks to redefine the roles of teacher and student. The legend attempts, by establishing personal concern for each student, to build a cooperative relationship rather than the adversarial one he or she may otherwise inherit if he or she just remains "teacher" and they remain "students." The legend makes learning seem like more of a joint effort, everyone pulling in the same direction. This attitude is possible only if the teacher has first reached out at an individual level to the students.

Approach 2: Take the We Approach

The second strategy for establishing a motivational foundation is to inaugurate "safety nets" for the students. Too many times we've heard teachers blame students for low scores, explaining that lack of success was a function of the students' lack of effort. Seldom do we witness teachers' sharing the responsibility for their students' progress or lack of it. Unfortunately, when a teacher's first reaction is to separate himself or herself from students' shortcomings, the newly proclaimed division is immediately obvious to the students, and such a segmentation is derisive in nature—not motivational.

> *The teacher interested in motivation should be prepared to compare himself or herself with the school's baseball coach. If the baseball team wins 6 games and loses 25, then its record is 6-25. But more important to us, that is also the coach's record.*

In the classroom, for some reason, teachers tend to distance themselves from their students' successes and failures as if their students' record were not their own. That distance becomes a gap so wide that it may never be bridged again, and, consequently, motivation becomes impossible.

The second step of building a foundation for motivation is for the teacher to abstain from separating himself or herself from the students and adopt instead a *we* approach to education. In the *we* approach to learning, the adversarial student-teacher relationship is replaced by a cooperative one. Poor test scores or performance will no longer be followed by power statements such as

- "What's wrong with you kids?" or
- "Boy, you really blew that one!"

Instead, they will be followed with comments such as

- "I thought I had prepared you better for the exam."
- "The scores show that we need a new plan of attack."
- "This is what we're going to do differently this time."
- "What suggestions do you have to improve the results?"

The *we* approach of shared responsibility to education takes as its focus success rather than blame. It allows teachers to pick up the pieces after a failure, while still safeguarding the dignity of students. By sharing in the responsibility for students' successes and failures, the legend has constructed a foundation on which motivation may be developed. No longer merely an external auditor, the teacher is a partner of learning, and that partnership inevitably leads to trust and respect—and that's when students can be motivated, for we want to please our friends, those we respect, those whose approval we desire. We care little about pleasing our adversaries.

Approach 3: Build Safety Nets

That leads us to our final step in establishing the foundation for effective motivation. This step is predicated on two major observations about today's students.

Observation 1

Many more of our students' lives are immersed in failures over which they have no control—failed relationships at home, failed jobs, failed health—than ever before.

Observation 2

Teenagers are the most insecure people in the world, their lives vulnerable to a host of different pressures: pressures about dating, pressures about drugs, pressures about gangs, pressures about parents, pressures about clothing, pressures about sexuality, pressures about race, pressures about grades . . .

The conclusion to be drawn from these two observations is that it is absolutely amazing that teenagers will agree to take any further risks at all; yet, the biggest risk any students voluntarily take is when they decide to try at school.

When they attempt to succeed in their classes, they have, in essence, placed their self-esteem on the line. While they are endeavoring to define themselves as adults, while they face all the pressures itemized above, we ask them to try to pass our courses. The legend, the masterful teacher, is sensitive to the nature of this request; the legend has not lost sight of the fact that adolescence is the most precarious time of people's emotional lives.

Keeping in mind this state of perpetual anxiety that defines teenagers, is it any wonder that so many have decided to drop out, at least emotionally, in terms of their effort? Therefore, the biggest and final step the legend takes to motivate students is to create safety nets so as to make the students less fearful of trying to succeed, less fearful of facing failure.

By high school, and unfortunately even by middle school in some cases, students' number one defense mechanism against feelings of inadequacy is to withdraw and make no attempt at success at all.

> *The teacher who wonders if motivation is a problem in her classes would be wise to take a self-inventory about her own concerns as a teacher.*
>
> *Q: What was my biggest concern at assessment time when I began teaching?*
> *A: Worry about students' cheating*
> *Q: What is my biggest concern at assessment time now that I've taught a while?*
> *A: Worry about students who don't care enough to cheat*

Can we blame them? As adults, how many of us regularly pursue activities at which we usually fail (other than golf and marriage)? The conclusion is remarkably clear—it is little wonder that so many of our students refuse to be motivated: Their fear of failure in what might be a world full of failure is far greater than their hope for success.

Their logic is quite obvious and sound: "If I don't try and subsequently fail, I haven't really failed because I never bought into the system; however, if I try and subsequently fail, I've failed because I'm inferior."

The fear of failure can, to a large degree and with most students, be countered by the creation of safety nets. After establishing strong personal relationships, after establishing a sense of shared responsibility, the legend is ready for the final step in motivating hesitant learners.

With safety nets in place, students are less likely to view failure as a personal reflection of their own shortcomings, less likely to fear failure. They are more willing to try in class, and that is what motivation is all about.

Safety nets come in two forms: attitudinal and systemic. (We both have been waiting for seven chapters to use the word *systemic*. Using it now is not only extremely satisfying, it's so very chic!)

Attitudinal Safety Nets

The premise of attitudinal safety nets was discussed previously—the focus of the class is in celebrating victories, not failure. Students' delicate self-esteem will be protected at almost all costs. Failures will not be publicized, they will be protected. If failure must be addressed, and of course it will have to be, it is at the conference level only—with strict confidentiality, and then in a positive manner, focusing on what can be learned from the failure and how it can be avoided in the future.

The safety nets themselves are taught as much as the material of the class. The legend stresses to students that temporary setbacks are a part of life and the class and need not be feared. The legend shows students that failure is a challenge—a chance for greater success. The legend has convinced students that they will not be humiliated when they stumble, and they will never be embarrassed if they have made a good effort.

Of course, as the students are quick to point out, talk is cheap. Attitudinal safety nets are really created by the teacher's execution of what he or she has assured students. If the teacher is sincere in wishing to protect students' feelings and demonstrates it repeatedly following every assessment, then the students will quickly appreciate and believe in the presence of these attitudinal safety nets. They will become risk takers, willing to give a real effort toward learning and success if, and only if, the teacher has essentially eliminated the psychological risk from that effort.

Systemic Safety Nets

After doing all that can be done emotionally to protect students from failing and, maybe more important, from fear of failing, the legend initiates a series of programs that either prevent students from failing or help them rebound if they do occasionally fail. Such programs may include, but are certainly not limited to, the following:

- Guaranteed passing grades for anyone who does all the work all the time at a suitable level of effort and caliber—a form of mastery learning
- Ungraded pretests that students must pass before being allowed to attempt the graded tests
- Mandatory make-up exams for students scoring below the C level (Special note: Neither of us is particularly fond of the concept of a D grade in the traditional scoring rubric. One either succeeds—A, B, C—or one fails—F. We view a D much like an educational coma—an unnecessary compromise of standards and expectations.)
- Compulsory and weekly review sessions for people with averages below the C level

The options are virtually endless and fully amendable to the concerns of the individual teacher, department, building, or district, but all are predicated on the belief that the first priority, the prime directive, in education is to see that the students master the material, that they learn. That is what teaching ought to be about.

Once the legend has built a foundation for motivation by establishing personal relationships with the students and communicating a sense of shared responsibility for success, then it is only a matter of sealing the covenant with the students by initiating programs that actually help them pass. All these safety nets are covenants with students indicative of the teacher's commitment to their success, proof that the teacher is working on their behalf. Then, and only then, may the teacher ask students to take a risk by trying to pass. That is the only motivation that matters.

ADDING GRAIN BY GRAIN

Successful motivation is not achieved with a single trick or concept. It is built one grain of trust and caring at a time. To that end, the legend is very much aware of the nuances implicit within the learning environment. He or she realizes that education is nothing more than a culmination of individual gestures. What follows are several of these gestures that any teacher can make. All are designed to develop strong personal relationships with students and to build safety nets for them.

Be Available

We begin by including our home phone numbers, e-mail addresses, Web sites, homework hotline numbers, and hours of availability on the very first course-orientation material or syllabus distributed. During the year, we encourage our students to call whenever they require assistance or simply need someone to talk to. Experience shows that students rarely use the opportunity to call a teacher at home, but when they do, tremendous motivation may be the consequence. In fact, even if no one were to use the option of calling during the year, by making the gesture the teacher has scored motivational points toward becoming a legend.

Give Cues

Prompts are a small technique that can be used to send the caring message of how deeply the teacher is committed to working toward the success of the students. During class work, there are two easy ways to get students to focus on important points. The first is through verbal clues given during the discussion or lecture. "This is important, get it down in your notes!" or "That would be a good test question!" are two examples of easy prompts for students to follow. Such prompts indicate to the students that there is more going on in the class than merely dispensing information. They also strengthen the impression that there is a team effort occurring and that the teacher's main concern is the success of the students.

Use Visuals

Another good technique is to become more visual in nature. When using the chalkboard, overhead, or handouts, the teacher can color code the information. This is a very effective method for targeting the important information whose use or recall will be measured later. For example, one could use black for ancillary material; blue for information that may be included on tests or quizzes; and red for material that most certainly will be on examinations later. Any such strategy serves two purposes: First, it is a motivational builder because it communicates continued caring and team effort. Second, it serves the very real function of teaching organization and prioritizing skills to the students. Any visual or mnemonic device helps the student process information in an orderly fashion, increasing everyone's likelihood for success later.

"But," you say suspiciously . . .

A few may complain that prompts and organizational hints are merely ways to spoon-feed students. Critics will maintain that students should have to determine on their own what is important when they are studying—that they need to learn everything before the test, not just what the test covers. Such critics accuse us of encouraging teachers to "teach the test."

To them, we reply by referring to our discussion of educational priorities. Complaints such as these come from people who believe their first priority as teachers is to sort students by grades, and we admit, nothing is more effective in accomplishing this than by giving no direction concerning assessment. Of course, when failing to do so, we by default end up sorting students not by what students could have learned about the topic under study but what they might have garnered based on the following:

- The study skills they already possess
- The past knowledge they brought to class
- The type of home lives they may have
- The degree of peer support they enjoy outside of class
- Their ability to intuit our intent

They have measured these aspects of the students' lives, but they have not measured what students could have learned, by what we might have taught them. When teachers give no direction toward assessment, when teachers choose to keep that information concealed, their tests measure note-taking skills, prioritizing skills, test-taking skills, but not necessarily what the curriculum suggests the students need to master. Teachers, therefore, are not that important in the educational process.

This trial-and-error approach toward learning is really a trial-and-failure approach, and as we suggested earlier in this chapter, many of our students today are not as emotionally prepared to learn by this method as perhaps we once were. It is an approach that not only fails to motivate but also destroys student initiative. The week before the school's football squad takes on its arch rival, no one accuses the coach of teaching the test when he has scouted the opponents and has the team scrimmage against the opponent's offensive and defensive formations. They do so to avoid surprises on the following Friday. We need to become our students' coaches.

Avoiding surprises on the test is a motivational tool for the teacher who is willing to be a student's coach. Preparing the students for what will be evaluated on the test and how it will be evaluated is only fair. Doing so enhances that feeling of mutual trust and respect so essential to any motivation. Approaching an examination with the Darwinian "Let's see who figured out what they were supposed to learn this unit and flunk those who didn't!" destroys the team concept of teacher and student working together. It creates an adversarial relationship—one definitely not conducive to motivation.

The legend helps students zero in on what is important. The legend helps students master basic knowledge and skills without obfuscating them. The legend does not teach the test. We are not suggesting a compromise of the principles we presented in Chapter 3, but the legend does teach "toward" the test. The difference is not slight; the line between the two is clearly unequivocal.

> *Motivational teaching:* "You will have to know the noble gases for the test."
> *Teaching the test:* "You have to know Helium and Neon."
> *Motivational teaching:* "You should know at least five causes of the Civil War."
> *Teaching the test:* "Memorize these five causes of the Civil War."
> *Motivational teaching:* "You will be expected to graph equations on the test."
> *Teaching the test:* "The answer to 12 is B."

The legend recognizes that time is a precious commodity for everyone today, including students. If students spend 2 hours studying important terms from Chapter 12 the night before an exam and then are tested on the graphics at the end of Chapter 13, they will quickly stop putting forth effort in that classroom. That teacher has reinforced students' nihilistic view of education (and life) to destroy any reason to be motivated at all.

These are just a few suggestions, but the concept is clear. To become a legend, a teacher must successfully motivate students. Motivation comes in the guise of strong personal relationships, shared responsibility for success, safety nets, and continued efforts to enhance the likelihood of success of the students to help them learn what is important in the class. It is built patiently one grain at a time; once destroyed, it may be impossible to reconstruct.

BUILDING ON THE FOUNDATION

The most important aspect of motivation after the legend has built the strong foundation and continues to add to it grain by grain is student success. As discussed at length in Chapter 2, success breeds success. Here are two bits of real observational genius:

- Seldom do students name as their favorite class one in which they are doing poorly.
- Everyone will succeed in something in school.

When the students sense that they cannot be outstanding in any school-sanctioned venue (i.e., academics, sports, extracurricular, popularity, socially), then they will go elsewhere, places we (and society in general) would prefer they wouldn't go.

The legend recognizes that every student should be able to succeed in the classroom and experience a sense of self-worth and importance through educational success. In fact, the elusive concept of self-esteem is really spelled S * U * C * C * E * S * S. The only way true self-esteem is built is through making people successful.

In turn, the implications for motivation are clear.

In becoming a legend and in motivating students, the teacher does everything in his or her power to ensure that students are successful.

> *This is accomplished at the very start of the school year by making sure that the first assignment is the type of assignment on which everyone can do well.*
>
> *Throughout every unit, work is incremental, beginning with exercises with which everyone can succeed.*

The legend recognizes the fact that students are motivated more by success than by failure. Students can be taken further if they are succeeding along the way then if the unit begins with an exercise that does little more than show everyone how little anyone knows. Grades should not have to be raised throughout a unit. They should begin high, and everyone's goal should be keeping them there. In many classrooms, unfortunately, this is not the case.

Another important blueprint for building on the foundation is twofold:

■ Student work must always be evaluated by the teacher immediately. It is hypocritical to enforce due dates for student work when the teacher can return graded material when he or she has time to get it done. Instead, knowing that work not returned within 48 hours has no learning value, the legend makes sure everything is returned the next day. The work is fresh in the students' minds, and learning can continue when the work is returned.

■ Likewise, class grades are regularly posted and updated. Both of these practices demonstrate the work ethic for the student and reinforce the shared responsibility approach in the classroom.

The teacher has shown, through both concerns, that he or she will work just as hard and responsibly as the students toward their success. This cooperative effort is motivational.

Regularly posting grades (e.g., once a week or after every major grade) serves another motivational function. If we truly expect students to take responsibility for their own learning and success, then they must know where they stand. Besides ending the guessing game about how students are doing, posted grades anonymously by code number shifts responsibility for progress onto students' shoulders. As the semester draws toward a close, students can see how well they must do to earn that grade they so much desire. Correctly or not, grades are students' paychecks, and students should know how much they're making and how often they will be paid.

In addition, they begin to develop a work ethic as they see how their grade is affected by success and failure. They can begin to form some direct correlations between hard work and better grades.

Getting work back to the students regularly the next day and keeping grades posted at least weekly are two strong motivational strategies that direct students to even more success.

Another motivational device is visual recognition of excellent work, as described Chapter 6. Repeatedly using visual recognition works motivationally in a very strong fashion. Almost every high school student can do a decent parody of rap music. They are able to do this not because all are musically talented, but because they are inundated with examples of rap music. So too does the legend inundate the classroom experience with examples of excellent work.

The last, and perhaps easiest, aspect of the educational environment that can be manipulated to increase students' motivation is the physical. Bulletin board displays, posters, walls of fame, and samples of good work are just a few of the many visual motivators that can surround students every day in class. In medieval times, the church realized that common man was not going to be able to follow the Latin mass and would spend much time in church daydreaming, so the church came up with the idea of stained glass windows. Such windows not only beautified churches but also depicted Bible stories to those whose minds wandered and who probably could not read.

In the same manner, the legend does not miss a chance to surround students with informative, interesting, motivating material relevant to class work. Anyone walking into the legend's room knows not only the subject matter of the instructor but also what unit is being studied. The walls are covered with posters, student work, inspirational phrases, and enrichment materials. The classroom itself becomes the teacher's aide. Such manipulation of the environment is yet another example of building on the foundation for motivation.

CONCLUSIONS

To become a legend, one must motivate students. Carefully groomed personal relationships, shared responsibility for success, and safety nets combined with numerous motivational strategies are key ingredients in winning students over to the teacher's side. As we stated at the outset of this chapter, there is no single, simple answer to motivation, no magic theory or secret strategy. What motivates is a visibly strong work ethic that allows the teacher to show the way by modeling successful work habits for the students. The legend communicates with students that he or she does care and is committed to their success. The legend repeatedly goes out of his or her way to do the little things that help make the student successful. Motivation doesn't begin with the students, it begins with the teacher, is shared by both, and is finally adopted by the students.

8

◈

DEVELOPING POWERFUL
CLASSROOM MANAGEMENT SKILLS

There remains finally the issue of control. Nothing thus far discussed matters if the teacher does not have control of the learning environment itself. The issue of control is a challenging one— some teachers are able to master control easily and others struggle their entire professional lives with it.

The fact of the matter is that classroom control could be, perhaps should be, a book unto itself, but what we try to do here is offer some positive comments based on our observations of the most successful teachers, the legends, for whom control never seems to be a real issue.

Perhaps what we offer can make a difference for others, enabling them to a make a difference for their students. After all, we are all teachers and we'd love to put the striped shirts and whistles away and someday just teach.

Originally, this chapter was going to be about pedagogy, but further consideration led us to the conclusion that pedagogy is really the concern of the clinician. Instruction about methods and styles abound in today's staff development field. Rehashing any of the current ideas on cooperative learning, mastery learning, effective school correlates, Socratic methods, or multiple intelligence seemed rather secondhand and definitely out of this work's focus. Instead, for our final view of the legend, we examine classroom management skills. For finally, it is the orchestration of the class that to a large degree determines success. To examine classroom management, we have divided the issues into four topics:

- Maintaining a student orientation
- Sustaining a learning environment
- Teaching how to learn
- Defusing threatening situations

MAINTAINING A
STUDENT ORIENTATION

Above all else, in the classroom the legend maintains an orientation exclusively aimed at student learning. Close examination suggests that to a degree, a component of the problems that plague education stems from a lack of direction, or more appropriately, from a confusion of direction. The nonacademic responsibilities thrust on the teacher are many and diffuse, but more important, the social concerns voiced most often by parents, administrators, and the popular press tend to cloud a teacher's real instructional objectives. Education is repeatedly held up as the panacea for every one of society's ills. If something is wrong in America, it can be improved initially (and most economically) through education. Thus, we are not surprised to find many teachers adrift when it comes to their true orientation. Our concerns in this area are best exemplified in the following personal experience.

When my son was a freshman in high school, he had a great deal of difficulty in his history class; his grade wavered between a C and a D. As the semester continued, I tutored him more and more at home. As one major test approached, we dedicated ourselves to his success on it. We studied long and hard. By the time of the test, we were both ready for it.

When he came home from school on test day, he reported rather optimistically he thought he had done well. The test was given on a Wednesday, so on Thursday and then on Friday when he said it was not yet graded, I wasn't too surprised. Even though, as we pointed out earlier, research has shown for years that only materials scored and returned within 48 hours have any learning value for the students, a wait of up to a week or two was not uncommon in my son's school.

Finally, 10 days later, my son returned home from school, rather dejectedly. With some shame he admitted he had earned a D. I was furious with him. What was his problem? Didn't he care about his grade? Didn't he see how this could affect his future? (Fortunately, I am much more rational as a teacher than I am as a parent.)

As I calmed down, he explained that he had really scored a B- on the test, but his grade had been lowered 14% for having failed to put his name on the first page, hence the D. My anger toward my son dissipated quickly, and I was soon on the phone making an appointment to meet with his history teacher.

Now, before I continue, let me admit that his teacher was a veteran teacher, held in solid esteem by school and colleagues. I have no doubt that everything she did was done with regard to values she had developed as a teacher in response to the overwhelming demands placed on all of us. She was caring and intelligent; and although I was sure she was wrong, I was certain she had tried her best to do what she thought was in the best interest of her students.

When I met with her, she was reluctant to let me see the test. She did not let tests out, she explained, because that would mean she would have to make new tests every year. When she finally relented and let me see the test, I noticed that not only had my son's grade been reduced from a B to a D for not putting his name on it, but the test had no blank on which to do so. My complaint about hidden agendas and my argument that no one was ever required to put one's name where there was no blank fell on deaf ears. I finally left—no longer as angry as I was sad. Here was a lady dedicated to her profession, making all the wrong decisions because she had lost what should have been her true orientation. Clearly, her priorities as an instructor had evolved into the following.

> Priority 1: Labor saving. More important than how well the students learned was maintaining a system that kept work for the teacher to a minimum. Tests could not be used as learning devices because that meant she would have to make new ones.

> Priority 2: Training students. In the teacher's mind, her first job was to train the students to be socially responsible. Following the rules about names was in her mind worth 14% of the entire test grade.

> Priority 3: Generating grades. It was evident by punishing my son's score that the teacher's job, as she saw it, was to sort the students by perceived abilities. Categorizing students by grades was more important than anything (except for the first two priorities).

> Priority 4: Teaching students. Somewhere, buried beneath all her other misguided priorities, lay her intent to teach the children social studies.

Every action in the sequence of events showed that student learning was, in reality, this teacher's lowest priority, the least important consideration in her hierarchy of duties. Our contention in this book is that the legend does not share these priorities and instead bases every decision on how it will affect student learning. Doing so accomplishes two things immediately:

1. It makes every decision eminently easier. All facets of a situation are now weighed against one orientation only—what is best to ensure that learning occurs. This absolute orientation to one priority simplifies a teacher's life considerably.

2. This orientation makes every decision much more defensible. Working backward as we have from a set of terminal outcomes, every decision in the class from curricular to disciplinary is now not only made, but is absolutely defensible in light of the orientation to learning.

The legend preserves this absolute focus on student learning. In the legend's class, all decisions are made from this orientation. Decisions regarding homework, seating, discipline, classroom routines, grading, group work—absolutely every aspect of the educational day—are made in light of this focus.

SUSTAINING A
LEARNING ENVIRONMENT

Once the teacher has assented to this absolute orientation to student learning, the next step is merely the logical extension of the first. The regulations and rules of the classroom must be determined only as they affect the learning environment. It matters not to which school of discipline one ascribes; what does matter is that every rule and regulation that drives the class has been clearly made with the learning success of the student in mind. This is turn has three major implications.

- First, every restriction of student behavior is justified only in terms of the degree to which that behavior would otherwise interfere with learning.

- Second, every punishment must be meted out only as it will affect learning positively later in the course.

- Lastly, every student must be convinced of the reality of the first two standards.

When rules and consequent punishments are designed and applied with these three standards in mind, then the number of discipline problems existing will quickly decrease. We would all do well to understand a basic truth about public education: Forget mandatory attendance laws, students are in school voluntarily. Need proof?

- It is ridiculous to believe that we could physically make 1,000 students attend school every day.

- It is equally ridiculous to believe that one teacher could make 20 junior or senior high students sit in a classroom and behave for 50 minutes.

The reality of the situation is that our command over the students derives from their voluntary submission to our authority. This voluntary behavior, therefore, indicates that to a very large degree they have already bought into the system and into the belief that getting an education will serve their best interests. If, in turn, they see every rule and every act of discipline performed for the sake of their learning, they will most certainly accept such actions more readily. On the other hand, behavior that does not interfere with learning (not social training, but learning) is, therefore, not the concern of the teacher or school.

A further word about discipline here, one that is more fully developed in the last section of this chapter: Every rule that is enforced and every disciplinary action that is carried out must be done dispassionately. Because the legend has already attempted to dispel any adversarial relationship between teacher and student, and because both rules and discipline are totally learning oriented, their enforcement is never accomplished in anger. Instead, they are done almost reluctantly at times, but they are done and they are done uniformly.

In addition to the simple rules and regulations for operating the classroom, a more important consideration is the emotional environment established. When one watches students enter the legend's classroom, one gets an overwhelming sense that the students shed emotional baggage at the doorway. The legend has succeeded in creating an "emotional safe zone" in the classroom. To have achieved this a number of steps must have been accomplished.

1. Students must have learned that the legend's classroom is not an arena within which they can build reputations by acting up or getting away with any prohibited behavior. They've learned everyone is treated equally and fairly, and because everything done in class is for their benefit, they and their peers begin to view misbehavior as being costly to them all. Because they get away with nothing, they soon stop trying, and the educational environment has moved one step closer to being an emotional safe zone.

2. Being wrong in the legend's classroom is not a sin. Being passive, being uninvolved is—but not being mistaken. In fact, the legend rewards risk takers for asking questions and venturing opinions. The

legend encourages active participation by rewarding it. Of course, the reticence of the shy student is recognized and respected, but shyness can be an incredibly debilitating handicap, and work must progress to overcome it. The legend's classroom makes such progress possible.

3. Students have learned that their self-esteem will not be threatened in this classroom. The legend is able to balance a degree of anxiety about learning with a larger degree of safety so that every student knows that he or she will not be humiliated as a form of discipline. Students know that everyone is equal in the legend's classroom. There are no favored students, and individuals are safe from emotional attacks by other individuals or groups. Likewise, the teacher himself or herself is as subject to teasing or joking as anyone is. Students quickly learn that they are valued in this classroom. Their opinions, their questions, and their presence are valued, and the legend makes them feel that from the beginning.

As a result of these steps, the students seem to discard their emotional defenses as they enter the legend's classroom. One senses students are almost relieved to enter this class, because here they can again be children without playing all the games of status that dominate their home lives and the social interactions with their peers. This sense of emotional freedom is the cornerstone to the entire concept of sustaining a learning environment.

TEACHING HOW TO LEARN

Once the teacher has oriented all classroom activities to student learning, there remains a final step, a last fine-tuning of all instructional activities, and that is the differentiation of what to know from how to learn it and how to use it.

The legend is concerned with the subject matter of instruction, but he or she is more concerned with the process of learning that occurs. Dispensing information to students, information that they should for some reason mysterious to them know, is not the practice of the legend.

As we have become more of a consumer-aware nation, we have found most professionals responding to our desire to be informed. Our dentists tell us step by step what they are doing and why. Doctors and nurses that used to hide our own charts from us now tell us fact by vital fact what they perceive and what they note. Even at the auto service department, careful records are kept of every transaction and attempts are made to keep those of us who are not mechanically challenged abreast of what needs to be done and why.

For some reason, however, education has not kept step with this trend. Teachers do not, by and large, spend enough time promoting their subject matter in real terms to the students. "Why do we have to learn this?" is a legitimate question, one that not only deserves an answer but that should be answered before it can be asked.

So we must construct a new approach to learning—one that accepts and responds to the feelings of the students prior to the dispensation of information.

Phase 1

Every new unit, every venue of instruction, should be preceded by a justification of its presence. The students are our clients and should be an integral part not only of the instructional process but to a degree its planning. Informed clients are much more likely to join the successful completion of the project voluntarily than disenfranchised students who have been asked to trust the system. The first step in teaching students how to learn is to teach them why they must learn. Only after they have acquiesced to this may the instructor successfully move on. In terms of the learning environment, students who have bought into the need to know will necessarily display better behavior and stronger effort.

One need only ask about the kinds of discipline problems the driver education teacher faces—the answers are obviously "minor and few." The reason is not that driver education teachers have different students; instead, it is that two of the most important premises of education have already been fulfilled:

- Driver education students know why they must learn the material.
- They want to learn it.

Although we may have trouble making cell mitosis as applicable to students' lives as driver education, we must try. Frankly, if we can't make it relevant to their lives, maybe we ought to rethink its role in our curriculum. For 50 years, research has told us that teaching standardized sentence diagramming in English does not improve students' reading or writing abilities; instead, it makes them better grammarians. Of the 120 students that the average English teacher sees in a day, how many will go on to become grammarians? Clearly, the first step in teaching learning is justification of the material to be learned.

Phase 2

Although the first step is relatively obvious, and almost every teacher is forced to accomplish it with a degree of regularity, we suggest that it be accomplished exuberantly and daily. (Okay, *exuberant* might be a little strong, even for us, but we can at least insist on *willingly*.) The second step is one that may be completely overlooked, and that is teaching the students how to learn the material. We'll make a blanket statement here, but one we believe we can stand behind. No material should be introduced without accompanying instruction on how to learn it. Such instruction should be logically constructed to fit the students' preexisting knowledge base. As much as possible, it should be experience referenced or kinesthetic in nature (because we remember that to which we can relate because of past experience and that which we move in space more than we remember things for which we do neither). As much as possible, it should be made concrete rather than abstract, specific rather than vague: Examples are more memorable than concepts. Let's take a look at some illustrations of this second step at work.

> To make learning experience based, one enterprising junior high biology teacher made arrangements with parents to bring students' pets in. The menagerie ranged from dogs and cats to lizards, turtles, birds, and fish. When each child was in a group where there was one pet, the directions were given: Identify things that the students physically had in common with the animals. Once these lists were completed and displayed so everyone could see them, the instructor categorized the animals

as either mammals or nonmammals. Then he announced that people were mammals. The students were then asked to identify those things they had found that were true of the animals that were mammals but not the nonmammals. The list they finally produced was the list of distinguishing characteristics of mammals. The 1-day project was used to teach the concept of scientific classification of living creatures along with the distinguishing features of mammals. The episode clearly related to past experience (it involved students' pets) and prompted their desire to learn.

When introducing a unit on non-Western stories, one English teacher began by dividing the class into five groups, each given identical scrap pieces of construction paper, scissors, and tape. Each was also given a set of directions indicating how to construct a model home from their materials. What they did not know was that each group was given one special direction. One group was told that good houses never had like color pieces of paper touching each other; another was told that the house should get progressively lighter in color the higher it went; another was told it should get darker. One was told all pieces should be cut into triangles and that all pieces should be taped only on the outside of the house. Once everyone was done, each group was asked to rate each house according to how well it followed directions. Of course, each group rated its house best, thinking all the others had violated significant directions, not knowing other groups had been given different directions. From this rating, the concept of differing values, morals, and taboos was introduced and the unit of non-Western stories began.

When first introducing stocks and the concepts of investment, one junior high teacher gave the students $1,000 in class money and told them to invest it in the stocks of their choice. The class then played the market for the next month. Students were told that their grades would be determined by how much money they had at the end of the project. Halfway through the unit, the teacher inserted brokerage fees for any transactions made. During the last week of the trading, the teacher began to leak information to a few students before trading on what the market was supposed to do that day. When others found out what was happening, the teacher introduced the concept of insider trading. (Once caught in his dealings, the teacher admitted that grades would not be determined by how much class money had been earned or lost.)

Such innovative techniques are not always available, obviously, but at the very least, the teacher needs to break down the intended skill into a set of behaviors that can be readily followed. One teacher taught sentence fragments and run-ons with this sequential method.

Step 1: Write down the number of independent clauses (ICs) indicated in a sentence by its punctuation.

Step 2: Find and label subject-verb combinations (SVs), each of which indicates a separate clause in the sentence.

Step 3: Identify ICs and subordinate clauses (SCs) knowing that all SCs are just ICs begun with a subordinating word.

Step 4: On the left hand hold up fingers to represent the number of ICs indicated by the sentence; on the right, hold up fingers to represent the number actually found.

Step 5: If the left hand equals the right, the sentence is correct. If the left hand is greater than the right, there is a sentence fragment; if the right hand is greater than the left, there is a run-on sentence.

Step 6: Correct the imbalance by changing the sentence to indicate more or fewer ICs or by increasing or decreasing the number of ICs present.

One teacher began with an examination of the 1998 Superbowl, where Green Bay was a prohibitive favorite to win over the Denver Broncos. Green Bay had the better defense, the better offense, the better record, more all-pro players. Everything that could be measured pointed clearly to a lopsided Green Bay victory. As we know, Denver did the unthinkable and won. How could this be? the teacher asked. Most students could offer some theories to explain the upset. Having finished with their responses, the teacher then introduced the concept of the Revolutionary War. How could the Americans have defeated the much more powerful British? The stage was now set for learning.

The point in all these examples is clear. The legend makes the material relevant to the students' world and teaches the student not only what to learn but how to learn it. Rather than worrying about the rapidity of learning, the legend is concerned with the quality of learning. In each example, the legend attempted to draw on what the students already knew to take the learning further. In all examples, the legend attempted to make learning kinesthetic, knowing that students learn more by manipulating their environment than by passively absorbing material. Each example shows a teacher attuned to how students most effectively learn.

The legend is especially sensitive to the feeling of defeat that students can experience when they don't learn. This feeling is quick to arise when students begin to sense that learning in a particular area is somehow intuitive, somehow an innate quality. That belief, of course, lies behind a student who says, "I never really got math!" It is even more solidly behind the parent who offers as an excuse, "Well, his father never could spell either." Both of these comments attest to the belief that certain types of learning are inherited, inborn, or congenital. The legend is the first to show the student that he or she can learn; teaching this is far more important than teaching what to learn.

This final concept is not at odds with the learning orientation discussed at the beginning of this chapter. What the legend knows is that by teaching students why they should learn and then teaching them how to learn, learning of the material itself will occur more quickly, more efficiently, and more permanently. The legend understands this nature of learning.

DEFUSING THREATENING SITUATIONS

One of the worst college professors we ever had surprised us one evening by making the observation that in almost every situation wherein a student erupted in class, the fault lay with the teacher. At first, because we had little respect for this professor, we were willing to reject this out of hand, but over the years, the wisdom of what he said has proven itself. It is our belief that in most situations in which student behavior becomes absolutely unacceptable, the main precipitating factor has been the teacher. Of course in today's troubled times, this is not always so: Teachers do not precipitate drug-induced frenzy, gang violence, or psychotic conduct, but they can be responsible for many of the other problems that interrupt learning in the classroom.

It is best to remember that we are speaking of any situation where a teacher must stop a behavior that is disruptive to learning and/or discipline a student. Anywhere along that spectrum lies the possibility of a student's violent outburst in response to the teacher's action.

This possibility of angered response exists largely because of five perceptions on behalf of the student. By addressing these perceptions, the teacher may greatly reduce, if not eliminate, the likelihood of a violent reaction from a student.

Perception 1: Inconsistency

The teacher has been perceived as being inconsistent. Because perceptions are more important than reality in situations like these, it is necessary that unmitigated objectivity is maintained in the application of discipline. Treatment of all students is open and according to set procedures. When new situations arise for which there are no precedents, no decisions are made until the situation has been thoroughly analyzed. (In other words, leave rash decisions to dermatologists.) Most important, to avoid the charge of inconsistency, rules and regulations must be applied to all students equally despite their reputations, well-earned or not. If Jose must have a pass to enter class late, so must Julie. If Joel may not use the washroom during class, neither may Latisha. Ever!

Perception 2: Unfairness

The teacher has been perceived as being unfair. One key to defusing this misperception is to have consequences for action clearly spelled out beforehand. Another is to involve the offender in the determination of the punishment. A third way is to have the punishment fit the crime: one minute late to class today—how about arriving a minute early tomorrow? A final approach is to make the punishment as rehabilitative as possible, rather than punitive.

Fundamental principles to make sure that discipline is not viewed as unfair:

- Punishment should not be associated with grades (that is a completely separate issue).
- Punishment should not be degrading in nature.
- Punishment should not be associated with more homework being assigned.
- Punishment should not be classwide for the misbehavior of one or two individuals.
- Punishment should not be done in the heat of anger; the student is far more likely to see it as unfair than if the punishment is meted out coolly by a rational teacher.

Perception 3: Humiliation

The third key to defusing possibly violent situations is to adhere to the precept that discipline is never to be demeaning, neither in the nature of the punishment nor in its delivery. If the student believes he or she is being humiliated, then he or she must defend himself or herself, and rightfully so. Humiliating the student is a ridiculous premise by which to modify behavior. Whereas good-natured teasing, even friendly satire or sarcasm, may have its place in the classroom, among friends, the confrontational situation is no place for any of those. Maintaining the correct, businesslike, dispassionate tone is everything in such a situation. Now is not the time to be sarcastic or even to try to use humor. It will be misunderstood.

Perception 4: Battle of Egos

The fourth key is really a summation of the first three, and it suggests that a disciplinary scenario is never to be perceived (by teacher or student) as a battle of egos. Behavior is not a negotiable item. Expectations of proper behavior have been spelled out early in the course and have been agreed on (or at least acquiesced to) by everyone, including the students. The legend realizes that control is as much based on prevention of problems as anything. He or she is sensitive to the feelings of the students and realizes that the only time students lash out is if they are backed into an emotional corner and emasculated. (Hence the fact that outbursts are more often tradition- ally committed by males.) The legend does not do emotional battle with the student, because emotional battles must end with either the degradation of the student or an emotional outburst.

Perception 5: Saving Face

The legend fully realizes how important the concept of "face" is to teenagers. If they perceive a teacher is attempting to rob them of their face, then they feel the teacher has stolen their self-esteem or forced them to try to defend it by attacking the teacher. There is no reason to follow this course of action. Instead, all issues of discipline are to be dealt with quietly, personally, without humor, and without public shame. We understand that it is a battle for many young teachers not to feel so personally threatened by students that they become emotionally involved in discipline situations, but it is a detachment that must be mastered if one is ever to be a legend.

The legend probably has many fewer discipline problems than other teachers; the legend's class is run more efficiently and more strictly than others. This efficiency and this strictness are not the result of the legend's ability to control students emotionally, but because in the legend's class, students know they are emotionally safe from harassment and they will be treated consistently, fairly, without shame, and with respect. Being respected is as important to the student as it is to the teacher.

CONCLUSIONS

No teacher can succeed in classroom management if orientation is not maintained toward student learning or if a learning environ- ment is not maintained. The opportunity for learning must exist as a requisite to learning. Once this is accomplished, then the legend begins by teaching the students why they must learn and how they are to learn. Merely teaching what to learn is no longer (if it ever was) an acceptable goal for teachers. To succeed today, learning must be divided into thirds: why it should be learned; how to learn it; and what it is.

Years ago, when computer-assisted education was first pioneered, its backers promised that one day teachers would be superfluous because computers would take our places. It is true that if our job were nothing more than to present the information to be learned, computers probably would be the vehicle of choice. Of course, dispensing information is not teachers' only job. Computers are not learning oriented; they do nothing to provide a learning atmosphere, and they certainly don't show why or how to learn. People can do all these, and the legend does.

9

BECOMING A LEGEND

We are totally committed to the efficacy of education. It is our belief, based on a combined 50 years of teaching, that the legend, as we have described him or her, can teach anyone anything. It is also our belief that becoming a legend, as we've described it, is a goal to be sought by every dedicated teacher. It is a win-win situation. By striving to become a legend, the teacher wins from the increased support from students, parents, and administration. Students win because they learn more and have more fun doing it. And, of course, the community wins.

How does a teacher know that he or she has attained legend status? As we suggested initially, success is a journey and not a destination, but a teacher might suspect he or she is on the right track if something like the following were to happen.

Several years ago, in early spring, a 15-year English teacher was standing outside the teacher's workroom talking with several other teachers when a senior (SW) came up, excused his interruption, and asked if he might have a minute of the English teacher's time. The teacher had coached the boy as a freshman on the baseball team and had had him in class for a semester when the boy was a sophomore, so he had no idea of what the boy wanted to talk about. Nonetheless, the teacher agreed, and the two went to his room. Once there, the conversation unfolded quickly.

> *SW:* Listen, I hate to bother you, but this will only take a second.
>
> *Teacher:* No problem. What can I do for you?
>
> *SW:* Well, I wonder if you've heard any of those rumors about what happened at that party last Saturday?
>
> *Teacher:* Yes, I did; some of the students were caught drinking, weren't they?
>
> *SW:* Yeah, that's right. Well, the word around school is that I was one of the ones picked up.
>
> *Teacher:* I hadn't heard that.
>
> *SW:* The thing is, I just wanted you to know—it isn't true. I wasn't there. I don't drink.
>
> *Teacher:* I'm glad to hear that, but I don't have anything to do with it . . .
>
> *SW:* I know, but it's important to me that you didn't think I was like that.
>
> *Teacher:* I don't.
>
> *SW:* Good, 'cause it matters to me what you think.

What is evident here is the respect that this teacher has earned at that school. We are life touchers, and to have touched a life that deeply is a great reward, one not possible in most professions. One needn't have taught too long before the letters from former students begin to arrive. They are never many in number, but they are enough to keep any teacher going.

As you strive to become a legend, we hope that your rewards grow as ours have. We hope you too receive those letters and notes from students, that you are the one students stop at the school to see years after they've matriculated elsewhere. We hope that some day each of you will be stopped by someone in a public place and be introduced to a significant other as, "This is the one, the teacher I've always told you about."

There are many things amiss with public education, and there are many drawbacks to becoming a teacher—but there are rewards too. Why become a legend, why dedicate a life to being a master teacher? Because we were called to teaching, because we love what we do, and because we are hopelessly lost in the belief that what we do matters—matters a lot. But you knew that, didn't you?

We hope that what we have said will make your professional life even more rewarding than it already has been. Thank you for reading our book, and thank you for being a teacher.

CORWIN
PRESS

The Corwin Press logo—a raven striding across an open book—
represents the happy union of courage and learning. We are a
professional-level publisher of books and journals for K–12 educators, and we are committed to creating and providing resources
that embody these qualities. Corwin's motto is "Success for All
Learners."